CULTURED FOODS
FOR YOUR KITCHEN

CULTURED FOODS
FOR YOUR KITCHEN

100 Recipes Featuring the
Bold Flavors of Fermentation

LEDA SCHEINTAUB

FOREWORD BY SANDOR ELLIX KATZ
PHOTOGRAPHS BY WILLIAM BRINSON

RIZZOLI
NEW YORK

New York · Paris · London · Milan

First published in the United States of America in 2014
by Rizzoli International Publications, Inc.
300 Park Avenue South
New York, NY 10010
www.rizzoliusa.com

Design by Jan Derevjanik
Edited by Chris Steighner and Martynka Wawrzyniak

2014 2015 2016 2017 / 10 9 8 7 6 5 4 3 2 1

Distributed in the U.S. trade by Random House, New York

Printed in China

ISBN: 9780789327451

Library of Congress Control Number: 2014931972

To my mother, who knows a good sour pickle,
and to sweet memories of my father,
who declared every dish I made
for him "the best ever"

CONTENTS

FOREWORD BY SANDOR KATZ

Welcome to the fermentation revival! Foods and beverages transformed by the action of micro-organisms are older than recorded history and integral to culinary traditions in almost every part of the world. Fermentation preserves food effectively and safely, making it an essential strategy for eating local in a temperate climate. Fermentation also makes food more digestible and nutrients more bioavailable, removes certain toxins from foods, and contributes additional nutrients, some of which have been found to have powerful therapeutic benefits. The live bacteria in those ferments not cooked after fermentation (live-culture ferments) are probiotic, helping to replenish and diversify our gut microbiota and thereby promote improved digestion, nutrient assimilation, immune function, mental health, and many other physiological processes.

Fermentation also creates compelling flavors. These flavors can be strong, and not everybody loves every flavor of fermentation. Many are what we describe as "acquired tastes," but they can become quite irresistible. Take a look around any gourmet food emporium and what you will see (and smell) are almost all products of fermentation. Most cheeses and cured meats are fermented. Soy sauce, fish sauce, and the vinegar found in most other condiments are fermented. Coffee, chocolate, and vanilla are fermented. Olives and certain styles of pickles are fermented. Bread is fermented, as are wines and beers. Flavors of fermentation are prominent not only in Western cuisines but around the world. I have been unable to find a single example of a culinary tradition that does not incorporate fermentation, and in many diverse locales ferments are essential everyday foods. According to one scholar of fermentation, one-third of the food that human beings consume has been transformed by fermentation before we eat it. These foods and the fermentation processes that produce them are so ancient that we do not know the exact origins of any of them. Yet creative home cooks, along with chefs in some of the world's most acclaimed restaurants, are applying these ancient processes to new ingredients, in new ways, adding new twists, and creating innovative and exciting flavor sensations.

Ferments are savored as delicacies, celebrated as sacraments, embraced as daily staples, and prescribed as remedies. Culture as we know it would not exist without the contributions of microbial cultures. Yet despite the widespread and longstanding importance of these foods and beverages, hardly anyone makes them anymore, thanks to food mass-production and the push for ever-greater convenience. Sadly, the strands of continuity—passing on from generation to generation the essential cultural information of how to make and use fermented foods—have largely been severed. At the same time, we have been brainwashed by the ubiquitous War on Bacteria, indoctrinated to view bacteria as dangerous, to the point where fermented foods and beverages are perceived by many as dangerous, especially the idea of making them in our home kitchens. Many people project their fear of bacteria onto the process: "How can I know I have good bacteria growing rather than *bad* bacteria?"

In fact, fermentation is extremely safe, and can be thought of as a strategy for food safety. According to the U.S. Department of Agriculture, there have been *no* documented cases of food poisoning traced to fermented vegetables. This suggests that the process of fermentation actually makes food safer, since every year there are food poisoning outbreaks caused by raw vegetables. Most of my work as a fermentation revivalist has involved reassuring people of the safety of the process and showing them just how simple it is.

Fermenting in your home kitchen to create unique delicacies and healing foods can be extraordinarily rewarding, but not everyone feels they have the time, space, or inclination to do so. Beyond actually fermenting food at home, whether we make them or buy them, many people have no idea how to use ferments or integrate them into our daily food preparation. That's where this book comes in. In *The Cultured Kitchen*, Leda Scheintaub makes it easy. This book is full of creative inspiration for people trying to figure out how to incorporate fermented foods and beverages into their daily food routines. Ferments can accent the flavors and heighten the nourishing potential of any meal, and this book has abundant ideas for using ferments at breakfast, lunch, and dinner—for snacks, desserts, and even cocktails.

Leda Scheintaub's descriptions, recipes, and methods are clear and concise. Her recipes are accompanied by gorgeous color photos. Just leafing through these pages will make your mouth water. And the recipes themselves are really just jumping off points, providing ideas for you to create your own unique delicacies using ferments, to bring the magic and health benefits of fermentation into every meal you serve. Once you begin to understand how easy it is to add flavor to any meal with the help of fermentation, the creative possibilities are quite literally infinite. Open this door of enhanced flavor and nutrition and a whole new culinary universe becomes possible. This book can be your passport to the fermentation revival.

SAUERKRAUT-MAKING SETUP:
Kraut board, pounder, and weights

INTRODUCTION
GET CULTURED

I make it a point to enjoy some measure of cultured foods most every day, with *enjoy* being the operative word. Health benefits aside, the highly developed flavors found in ferments are a delight to good food lovers. Chocolate, coffee, tea, bread, cheese, beer, and wine are fermented foods that we are all familiar with. And once our taste buds get familiar with fermentation that goes beyond the everyday into the realm of the tart, tangy, sour, and umami flavors of kimchi, kefir, umeboshi, and beyond, they start crying for more. Fermentation becomes a welcome compulsion.

STARTING SMALL
(IN A TINY NYC APARTMENT)

One of my first attempts at home fermentation was sauerkraut. In my enthusiasm I laid out a hundred dollars for a dedicated three-gallon ceramic crock for making my own, but soon learned that there wasn't enough room in my studio apartment for both me and the crock *plus* the large bucket required to pound down the multiple heads of cabbage needed to fill that crock up. Not to mention the slight sauerkraut aroma perfuming my place, deliciously pungent but something I wasn't keen on living in the same room with 24/7.

An easier foray into the craft of culturing came with the fermented milk drink kefir, by some accounts the secret of longevity for the people of the Caucasus. Though the Russians may have been enjoying kefir for the past two thousand years, when I first was introduced to this beverage a decade and a half ago by my mentor Rebecca Wood, whose work in the field of health and healing has always been ahead of the curve, it was still a long way from becoming the next big thing in probiotics and a rival to yogurt. I ordered my kefir starter by mail. When the small package arrived, I popped the starter into some milk, let it sit overnight, strained it, and I was on my way to becoming a home fermenter. It felt good to know that this little bit of

alchemy could be pulled off right at home, and with each glass I would feel good, the energy from the kefir flowing directly into my system. (In fact the word *kefir* translated from the Turkish means "to feel good.") My kefir starter multiplied with every batch, and so with fervor I'd share kefir babies with friends, along with a simple set of instructions I'd written up, and hope that they would become kefir converts too. These were the early days of the local foods movement, and fermenting milk found at the farmers' market down the street felt pretty local for a city girl like me. Making kefir was something I was able to pull off easily, tidily, and conveniently in my elevator-size New York City kitchen.

With kefir I fell in love with fermentation, and I realized that I didn't have to become a total back-to-the-earth or DIY person to enjoy cultured foods. I could bring culture into my decidedly urban lifestyle by learning how to read labels, shopping for live cultured foods, and incorporating ferments into my recipes. I would buy my sauerkraut, kimchi, fermented hot sauce, and very active yogurt from a favorite Union Square farmers' market stall, while continuing to make my countertop kefir from local milk. I would learn that a good number of natural-food-store items—tempeh, apple cider vinegar, umeboshi plum vinegar, and miso, to name a few—were already fermented (and these days many supermarkets carry these once-labeled-as-health-food specialty products). I also would learn which label indicators assured me that the food was in fact naturally fermented and not pasteurized or otherwise processed.

I was happy to find that fermentation was perfectly in sync with life on the go in New York City. And years later when I moved to a Vermont home with a bigger kitchen and dedicated pantry (which houses my sauerkraut crock), I would make more of my own ferments but still often buy sauerkraut, kimchi, yogurt, kombucha, and the like from the local food co-op and farmers' market vendors. With so many homegrown options, I am curious as to the individual flavor of the different ferments and almost always give in to temptation when a new variety is on offer. Then I take my find, open the lid, relish in the delicious celebration of life, and dream about new recipes.

GETTING HOOKED ON FERMENTS

On a typical day I'll wake up and see what's creating new life on my kitchen counter or in the pantry. How thick is the crème fraîche? Is the kefir tangy enough? Have the pickles soured to my liking? Do I have enough kimchi to make kimchi pancakes for lunch? I'll have my breakfast, most often a fried egg slathered with fermented hot sauce, homemade or my favorite store-bought brand, followed by some sauerkraut to give a tangy sense of completion to the meal. A between-meal snack might be a glass of kefir, lunch is that kimchi pancake with a salad tossed in miso or pickle juice dressing, and dinner perhaps a classic cultured burger with all the fixings.

I enjoy a fermented vegetable with most of my meals to round out the flavors and textures, and I'm especially grateful for them when I'm needing a quick meal or looking to brighten up yesterday's leftovers. Adding a side of sauerkraut, for example, brings new excitement to last night's dinner, and kimchi stirred into reheated rice makes an effortless lunch. Dessert is a cultured scoop of kefir ice cream, granita, or berries

marinated in kombucha. Not every meal features ferments; I list these examples to simply show that it's easy to add culture to your life at any time.

In the pages that follow, first I'll give a brief background on fermentation and touch on its cultural roots and health benefits, then I'll show you how to shop for store-bought ferments, get your kitchen set for fermentation, and introduce you to my seven building block ferments: sauerkraut, kimchi, cucumber pickles, root vegetables, yogurt, kefir, and kombucha. Then the culinary adventure begins: We'll take our ferments into the kitchen and incorporate them into recipes in both familiar and not-so-familiar ways, some super-simple and others more complex, but all full of flavor, full of vitality.

AN ANCIENT CRAFT AND A HOT NEW TREND

Probiotics is a buzzword; people are starting to understand the importance of getting good bacteria into our daily food for digestive and overall good health. We're reaching beyond the standard yogurt and acidophilus supplements and looking to the past, a past in which our ancestors fermented cabbage, cucumbers, soy, coconut, grains—you name it—to keep themselves alive and thriving. Since before recorded history cultures around the world have incorporated fermentation into their culinary worlds, from sauerkraut in central Europe to kimchi in Korea, dosas in India, miso in Japan, and pickles in the United States. In Iceland they bury shark and ferment it to a state of extreme stinkiness; this sort of thing gets the attention of TV personalities (Anthony Bourdain called it "the single worst, most disgusting and terrible tasting thing" he'd ever eaten), but fermentation historically is an unassuming art. It is simply a method of food preparation and preservation and a way to make food more flavorful.

History was interrupted as we transitioned to an industrialized food system. Fermentation was never a large-scale type of food production (as you'll learn, part of the beauty of fermentation is that no two batches taste exactly alike), so standardization methods such as pickling with vinegar instead of salt were introduced. Canning and pasteurization became the new science, and hygiene became a cultural obsession. Frozen-food trucks allowed the delivery of once-regional products across the country. Food became shelf-stable and often longer lasting, but these modern versions of pickles, sauerkraut, and such lacked the vitamins and enzymes that natural fermentation gives a food, undoing thousands of years of tradition.

Sad as this story is, the good news is that traditional foods are enjoying a revival. Sally Fallon's *Nourishing Traditions* has been inspiring an ever-growing following of people, myself included, to question the modern food system and return to the culinary traditions of our ancestors. (Fallon's work has informed some of the recipes in this book.) We are also seeing a resurgence in artisanal food producers, a local foods movement with a thriving farmers' market culture, and a growing interest in fermentation as both home craft and big business, with multiple online sellers of fermentation crocks, kombucha mothers, and kefir cultures and natural food market cases dedicated to kombucha, kefir, pickles, sauerkraut, miso, and other ferments.

This is not just because these foods are traditional; it also comes from the recognition of the sophisticated nature of ferments. Cutting-edge restaurants are going beyond the fermentation standards—cheese, bread, and wine—to explore live-culture fermentation, and nowadays it's not unusual to see salt-brine pickles or kimchi on restaurant menus, kombucha on tap, and surprises like pistachio miso cashew tamari from David Chang's East Village fermentation lab, where the chef (of Momofuku fame) is searching out a "microbial terroir," giving a whole new meaning to the word *local*. This is new and exciting territory! It appears our culture is ready to learn from the past and is creating new traditions, all based on the transformation that is fermentation.

THINKING WITH YOUR GUT

So what does this transformation involve? There are several excellent books and blogs dedicated to the science of fermentation, the specific health issues fermentation can target, and what certain bacteria do for you once they enter your system. It's a fascinating study, and in the resources section I'll refer you to my favorite sources for further research if you'd like to get more into the subject. But my task at hand is to tempt you with a few good reasons to include fermented foods in your diet, and then invite you to get into the kitchen to try out my hundred recipes that put fermentation at the center of the plate.

Sandor Katz, who has inspired the most recent movement of home fermentation with his books *Wild Fermentation* and *The Art of Fermentation*, defines fermentation as "the transformative action of microorganisms"; bacteria and yeasts feed on the nutrients in food, which creates lactic acid, a preservative, and in doing so transform the taste and sometimes texture of the food. The results: cabbage into sauerkraut, tea into kombucha, milk into kefir. While fermentation has historically been a means of food preservation, it is also a way of getting maximum nutrition from food. You start with an already healthy food—say, carrots, coconut, or cucumbers—and then, through a culturing agent such as salt or whey (I'll go over those shortly), friendly bacteria are produced, bringing to that food even more living qualities. It's nothing short of a miracle of life.

As these friendly bacteria help us break down food and absorb nutrients, we're doing good not just for the digestion but for the whole mind-body system. According to Dr. Michael D. Gershon, author of *The Second Brain*, there is a strong connection between digestion and the brain, with 95 percent of the body's serotonin housed in the gut, and anxiety, depression, and other psychological conditions connected to digestion in ways we wouldn't have suspected. According to digestion expert Brenda Watson, the gut is the first line of defense against pathogens and toxins leaking into the bloodstream, and when the

Staying Alive

A guiding principle of my ferment-centered recipes is to keep the ferments live from start to finish (rather than cooking them to death) so they retain the good bacteria and beneficial enzymes they had when they went into the mix.

This comes naturally in raw recipes such as the Kale and Beet Salad (page 92) and Poseidon Salad (page 96), but in recipes involving cooking, a little creativity comes into play. For example, my Butternut Squash, Sauerkraut, and Hot Sausage Soup (page 107) veers from the traditional eastern European style of simmering the sauerkraut with the rest of the ingredients; instead the kraut is added after the soup is removed from the heat. The same goes for the pickles and yogurt in my Summer Chowder (page 112) and the miso paste in my Basic Miso Soup (page 104). Following the same simple concept, the kimchi in the Crunchy Kimchi Pork (page 149) is stirred into just-cooked pork, and the crème fraîche and cultured mustard are whisked into the Pickled and Smothered Pork Chops (page 158) pan juices after the heat is turned off.

Equally important to my cultured recipes is taking advantage of the wide range of flavors offered by fermentation, and naturally sometimes this is best achieved through cooking. Although the probiotics are reduced or eliminated when a food is heated, the inherent nutrition in the food is retained, and often deliciousness is increased. Still, I'll often add an element of live culture to these recipes for good measure; for example, I finish my Cheesy Kimchi Pancakes (page 122) with a sprinkling of raw kimchi, and while the ferments for the Hot and Sweet Wings (page 128) are used as a marinade and then get baked into the chicken, I dip the hot wings into a Gorgonzola dressing based on kefir for a final uncooked flourish.

When it comes to frozen desserts, if you start with a probiotic-rich kefir, yogurt, or crème fraîche, you'll end with an equally lively frozen treat, as freezing doesn't alter the beneficial bacteria.

gut is not at its best it can lead to seemingly non-gut afflictions such as chronic fatigue syndrome and other autoimmune disorders. Since fermented foods are partially digested before they even enter your mouth, when you include them in your diet your digestion, and as a result your whole body, is poised to be working at its best. Something to think about the next time you have a "gut feeling"!

Coming from the antibacterial culture we live in, it's understandable that we'd be skeptical about leaving a food on the counter unrefrigerated for days on end—won't it rot? Probably not, but you'll know if it does. If it's rotten, it will smell bad and you'll toss it out, just like you do when you come back from vacation and are reminded that you forgot to clean out the crisper drawer before taking off. If a small amount of mold forms on top of your ferment, you can scoop it off, confident that the brine or other medium will keep the invaders from making it into the ferment. Fred Breidt, a microbiologist with the U.S. Department of Agriculture, believes that properly fermenting vegetables is a safe practice, as there is little danger of exposure to harmful bacteria because the lactic acid bacteria that carry out fermentation are the world's best killers of other bacteria. There's a reason friendly bacteria got their name.

Other benefits of fermented foods: They can boost the immune system, function as antioxidants, and create omega-3 fatty acids. In dairy, fermentation transforms the lactose in milk into easier-to-digest lactic acid. In grains, fermentation neutralizes antinutrients such as phytic acid, making the grains easier to digest. Fermentation increases nutrition and creates new nutrients, including the B vitamins folic acid, riboflavin, niacin, thiamin, and biotin. Enjoying ferments means you can pass on costly probiotic supplements in favor of delicious food. If ferments aren't always going to be a staple, consider leaning on them during cold and flu season or after a round of antibiotics to boost your immunity. Just remember this: When you ferment a food, it will be healthier and tastier than it was before!

How much to eat? Traditional societies took in small amounts of fermented foods several times a day, often with meals. In this book we'll be making them *part* of our meals, so this should be easily accomplished. And when you're not making a specific ferment-centered recipe, a simple spoonful or two of sauerkraut with your meal, a pickle alongside a sandwich smeared with fermented mustard or ketchup, a midafternoon kefir break, or the like will ensure that you get your fill of culture in a most enjoyable way. Consider eating a variety of ferments for the greatest diversity of beneficial bacteria rather than a more-is-better approach; recent studies indicate that the more biodiversity you have in your gut, the less likely you are to have chronic illness and the more likely to enjoy overall good health. How inspiring that the delightful and diverse tastes found in fermentation are also supremely nourishing superfoods!

Six Good Reasons to Eat Fermented Foods

HEALTH: Probiotics are good for the gut, brain, and whole system. Probiotic supplements can be costly and vary in quality, so the best way to get your probiotics is by eating naturally fermented foods. Natural health insurance!

THRIFT: A head of cabbage is a lot cheaper than a jar of acidophilus capsules.

LOCAL AND SEASONAL: Putting up spring, summer, and fall produce for fermentation preserves the bounty of the seasons, allowing you to eat local all year long.

CONVENIENCE: Vegetable ferments have a long refrigerated shelf life—often up to a year or longer—and starters can last forever, so it's easy to keep your ferments on hand for a quick bite or inclusion in a recipe at any given moment.

TASTE: Fermentation develops the flavors of food, making cultured foods elevated ingredients to add to your recipes.

TRADITION: Folks have been fermenting since before recorded time for all of the above reasons; let's keep this important tie to our past going!

A Gift That Keeps Giving

Looking for that certain something for the friend who has everything? Give the gift of fermentation! There's something for everyone, from newbies to the culturing curious to those steeped in the craft. Here are some ideas to get you started:

POTLUCK PICKLES: A jar of sauerkraut, kimchi, or pickles (pages 23 to 33) spiked with your signature seasonings makes a great host gift.

HEIRLOOM YOGURT: A jar of yogurt made from your personal starter is a powerful present for someone who has always wanted to make her own yogurt (page 34).

BEYOND BUBBLY: A bottle of beet kvass (page 61) or fruit kvass (page 60) is the perfect nonalcoholic beverage option and a great conversation starter.

SPREADING THE LOVE: A jar of homemade mustard cultured with pickle juice (page 73) is one of the more unique presents you can give and a jar of Miso Parmesan (page 85) or a log of All-Around Almond Cheese (page 84) is a godsend gift for the dairy-free among us.

STARTERS FOR STARTERS: Look for online companies such as Cultures for Life for kits that include everything you need—from starter to strainer to container—for a specific ferment such as yogurt, kefir, or kombucha.

A MOTHER FOR ALL: Since a kombucha "mother" gives birth to a "baby" with every batch and kefir grains multiply quickly, you can share them far and near and join the worldwide web of culture sharing. Think of it as a gift that keeps giving.

Now it's time to get creative with packaging: Country-chic Ball jars and Kerr jars are always appropriate; smooth-sided glass jars made by Weck add sophistication. A decorative and informative label, perhaps a personalized one from your kitchen, can really make the gift special (a search through Etsy will give you multiple options), and don't forget the ribbon and bow!

GETTING SET FOR FERMENTATION

Here's where we'll get into readying your kitchen for fermentation, learn how to shop for ferments, and set the stage for a culinary adventure.

MY FEATURED FERMENTS

Cheese, bread, beer, wine, coffee, tea, and chocolate. Nations of good food have been built on these ingredients and entire books written on each of them. They are all fermented. However, sometimes these delicious foods do not retain their live cultures due to processing methods. Some of these foods can be found in my recipes as ingredients, but none is featured as a ferment. The ferments I've chosen to highlight are live, with their active cultures intact. Exceptions are tempeh and a few grains that are cooked, in which case the function of fermentation is to make them more digestible and nutritious, and then there are cooked foods like tomato paste, which we bring back to life by activating it with a fermentation starter to turn it into ketchup. Often the goal is to keep fermentation-centered recipes live start to finish (see the Staying Alive sidebar, page 14), and always to take advantage of the varied flavors of fermentation.

> As many of us are at our best when we avoid gluten, the recipes in this book are gluten free.

While some natural ferments are strictly DIY, many can be found in natural food stores and some supermarkets. My local food co-op has a whole refrigerator case dedicated to natural pickles, sauerkraut, hot sauce, miso, and the like. All you need to know is how to read a label to be assured the product in question is naturally fermented. (Hint: Two of the most common words to look for are *raw* and *unpasteurized*, and choosing organic when possible is always a good idea.) You won't be cheating if you use store-bought ferments in your recipes; in fact you will be supporting a thriving new business model rather than the industrial food complex. Opposite is a shortcut guide to get you going as you walk through the market aisles and set up a fermentation-friendly kitchen.

HOW FERMENTATION WORKS: A BRIEF OVERVIEW

There are three terms you'll often run into when reading fermentation recipes: *wild fermentation, lacto-fermentation*, and *culturing*. Fans of Sandor Katz's *Wild Fermentation* will be reminded that the eponymous term refers to fermentation based on organisms spontaneously present in the food or environment. When lactic acid bacteria are involved, as in the case of milk or vegetables, the process is known as lacto-fermentation (note that this process does *not* create lactose). When a starter such as kefir grains or a kombucha mother is added to initiate the fermentation process, it is known as culturing. Sometimes the distinctions overlap, and often in this book the terms will be used interchangeably.

What can you ferment? You may be surprised at the number of foods that take to fermentation. When it comes to vegetables, it goes beyond cabbage and cucumbers to carrots, asparagus, cauliflower, sweet and hot peppers, and just about everything else.

Shopping for Basic Ferments

APPLE CIDER VINEGAR

Vinegar made from crushed apples or cider

WHAT TO LOOK FOR: The words *raw* or *unpasteurized* or *with mother* (a cloudy substance at the bottom of the bottle).

CUCUMBER PICKLES*

Fermented cucumbers

WHAT TO LOOK FOR: The words *raw* or *unpasteurized*, containing salt rather than vinegar, refrigerated rather than from the grocery aisle; search out local and organic brands.

FISH SAUCE

Liquid made from salting fish, usually anchovies or sardines

WHAT TO LOOK FOR: No special label, but avoid brands that contain additives, as they can interfere with fermentation (you'll find it in Asian food stores).

KEFIR*

Cultured milk beverage

WHAT TO LOOK FOR: The words *contains live cultures*; favor unsweetened.

KIMCHI*

Spicy Korean-style fermented cabbage

WHAT TO LOOK FOR: The words *raw* or *unpasteurized*, refrigerated rather than from the grocery aisle; search out local brands.

KOMBUCHA*

Fermented tea beverage

WHAT TO LOOK FOR: The words *raw* or *unpasteurized*, from the refrigerator case.

MISO

Fermented soybean paste

WHAT TO LOOK FOR: The words *raw* or *unpasteurized*, from the refrigerator case, no dried miso in packets.

PRESERVED LEMON*

Lemons preserved in salt and lemon juice

WHAT TO LOOK FOR: A jar from the refrigerator case containing just lemons, salt, and seasonings; favor organic, as you will be eating the peel (Middle Eastern groceries carry it).

SAUERKRAUT*

Fermented cabbage

WHAT TO LOOK FOR: The words *raw* or *unpasteurized*, refrigerated rather than from the grocery aisle; search out local brands.

TAMARI

Naturally fermented soy sauce

WHAT TO LOOK FOR: The words *traditionally made*.

TEMPEH

Fermented soybeans formed into a cake

WHAT TO LOOK FOR: Tempeh is a cooked ferment, so there are no active cultures; look for organic to avoid genetically modified soybeans.

UMEBOSHI PLUM

Japanese salted plum

WHAT TO LOOK FOR: Packages of whole plums, paste, or vinegar in natural food stores or Japanese markets.

YOGURT*

WHAT TO LOOK FOR: The words *contains live cultures* and with no stabilizers or gums; favor unsweetened; search out local brands.

* Look for the DIY recipe in this book.

Seaweed can be fermented, and it makes a great accent to a jar of sauerkraut. Fruits can be fermented into fizzy drinks, chutneys, salsas, and sauces. Milk, nuts, and coconut can be fermented into kefir and yogurt. Grains can be fermented by soaking them in water with a starter. Meat and fish can be fermented (with the exception of a quick salt-cured salmon recipe on page 129, these two aren't in the scope of this book). Condiments, either homemade or store-bought, can be fermented to increase their nutrition, shelf life, and deliciousness. Few foods *can't* be fermented.

How can you create the best environment to nurture your ferments? The keys to successful fermentation are correct temperature, time, encouragement, and protection.

- Room temperature is usually the ideal temperature, and you'll want to keep your ferments away from sunlight.

- Timing can vary: Some ferments, such as kefir and crème fraîche, take just a day; sauerkraut can take a week or more; and preserved lemons ferment for a month. In warmer climates or seasons, fermentation time will often be shorter—it's a science but also an art, and after a few go-rounds you'll start to get a feel for when your ferments have reached the perfect stage of tanginess.

- Encouragement means feeding the food to be fermented a starter such as kefir grains, whey, or a kombucha mother or keeping it submerged under a salty brine.

- Protection involves keeping mold away from your ferments by monitoring them daily, stirring when needed, promptly removing any mold that does form on top (if mold penetrates below the surface, it's time to compost that batch), and trying to let go of the prefermentation antibacterial nation way of thinking that your food has spoiled: You've created an anaerobic environment in which it is almost impossible for bad bacteria to take root. It also means setting your fermentation jar on a saucer or plate to catch potential overflow and covering it with a cloth to prevent invaders such as bugs from entering.

What signs will tell you when it's ready? A bubbly surface, an indication of a happy culture. A change in color, comparable to when a food goes from raw to cooked. A lively smell—deliciously sour, perhaps a little yeasty or alcoholic, but never funky. As I've mentioned, if it's gone bad, you'll know it and you'll toss it. Taste your ferment along the way to tell if it's done; Sandor Katz recommends eating from your ferments at different stages of doneness to get the greatest diversity of flavors and good bacteria into your body.

This is just a brief overview; we'll go into more detail on these points in the recipes that follow, as each ferment has its own individual TLC requirements.

HOME FERMENTATION TOOLS

Do you have sea salt and a few glass jars lying around your kitchen? If the answer is yes, then your kitchen is ready for fermentation! Start simple, and then if you get more into the DIY aspects of fermentation (remember you don't have to make your own to complete most of the recipes in this book), explore your options: ceramic crocks, stone weights, airlocks, and the various home fermentation kits you'll find online.

Before we get to the setup, let's talk about cleanliness. We've learned that there are good bacteria and there are bad bacteria. To encourage the good bacteria to ferment our foods successfully, we want to keep competing (bad) bacteria away from our jars, crocks, utensils, and countertops, so anything that touches our ferments should be super-clean. Unlike canning, equipment doesn't need to be sterilized; a wash in the dishwasher or by hand and letting your jars completely air dry is enough.

VESSELS: Start with pint, quart, and half-gallon mason or other glass jars. Ceramic crocks are great for making large batches of sauerkraut and pickles, and there are many beautiful options to choose from (see Resources, page 183). Don't use reactive metals (like aluminum), and avoid plastic, unless it is food-grade and BPA-free. I do like to replace the metal lids that come with mason jars with plastic lids, as salty brine eventually rusts a metal lid; I save metal lids for travel, as they create a tighter seal than the plastic.

WEIGHTS: If you buy a crock, it may come fitted with a stone weight used to submerge the food under its brine to keep it in an anaerobic environment. If it doesn't or you're using a jar rather than a crock, you might try a drinking glass filled with water or a plate topped with a weight such as a rock or a zip-top plastic bag filled with brine (if the bag breaks, brine rather than water will fall into your crock and the salt-to-liquid ratio won't be compromised); any clean weight that covers the food and keeps it submerged will work.

AIRLOCKS: Home fermenters have started to borrow from the home-brew crowd by using airlocks, science-lab-looking inserts to container lids that enable carbon dioxide gases to escape without letting in air, preventing undesirable bacteria from coming into contact with your ferment. Our ancestors didn't have these, but some modern folk feel more confident using them. See Resources (page 183) for where to get them.

UTENSILS: A pounder for turning cabbage into sauerkraut is a handy tool; a meat mallet, large pestle, or potato masher can also do the trick. Mesh strainers are for straining kefir. Bottle cleaning brushes are helpful if you're making and bottling probiotic drinks. A wide-mouth funnel (the kind that's used for canning) is invaluable for tidily fitting vegetables into fermentation jars.

STORAGE: Your ferments will go into the refrigerator when they are finished, either in the jar you fermented them in or transferred from a crock into smaller jars. Beverages can go into jars too (you can reuse vinegar bottles, hot sauce bottles, and so on), and if you're bottling kombucha or other naturally fermented drinks to carbonate them, you might want to invest in Grolsch-style bottles with stoppers. These bottles are made of strong glass and are recommended to limit the chances of an exploding bottle. Or you could simply use recycled plastic water or juice bottles.

KITCHEN TAPE AND MARKERS: Label and date your ferments. You'll thank yourself later.

SALT BRINING

In many ferments such as vegetables, salt is used to create an acidic environment and keep bad bacteria out. Use only sea salt; I like fine unrefined sea salt because it dissolves easily. Table salt generally contains additives that can interfere with fermentation. Sometimes a food that's being prepared for fermentation is dry salted, meaning salt is rubbed into the food to start to break it down and begin fermentation. Sauerkraut (page 23), for example, employs this method. Another way of using salt is making it into a brine and pouring the brine over the food, as is done for cucumber pickles (page 28). Always use filtered water for your brine, as the chlorine in tap water can interfere with fermentation.

BASIC SALT BRINE

Makes 2 quarts (2 liters)

Many of my recipes call for salt brine; I recommend making a big jar of it and keeping it handy in the refrigerator. You may try out lesser amounts of salt if you'd like, but be aware that there's more chance of bad bacteria entering when you reduce the salt and the resulting ferments tend to be less crisp.

2 quarts (2 liters) filtered water

5 to 6 tablespoons fine sea salt

In a small saucepan, combine 2 cups (480 milliliters) of the water and the salt and bring to a simmer. Set aside, stirring occasionally, until the salt is dissolved. Pour into a glass jar and add the remaining 6 cups (1.5 liters) water. Cover and store in the refrigerator, where it will keep indefinitely.

STARTER CULTURES

Some fermented foods such as sauerkraut and kimchi need no added starter cultures, but many other ferments do require or benefit from a starter culture. Individualized starter cultures such as kefir grains for making kefir and a kombucha mother for making kombucha are not optional. Whey, the liquidy part that's left after straining yogurt or kefir, is often used as a jump-starter for ferments. Whey allows you to reduce the amount of salt in a recipe by about one third, which can be helpful when you don't want your ferments to taste salty, as with fruit chutneys and applesauce. Note that you could make a recipe with all whey and no salt, but a mushy texture is often the result. A loose rule of thumb is ¼ cup (60 milliliters) whey for each quart (liter) of ferments. Here's a basic recipe, but you won't really need it; every time you make a batch of Greek yogurt (page 37) or kefir cream cheese (page 40) you'll handily find yourself flush with whey.

WHEY STARTER CULTURE

Makes about 2 cups (480 milliliters) whey, plus about 2 cups (480 milliliters) Greek yogurt

1 quart (1 liter) dairy yogurt

Line a large strainer with a double layer of cheesecloth or a clean handkerchief (a double thickness of paper towels will do in a pinch) and set it atop a bowl. Pour the yogurt into the cheesecloth and tie the ends up. Refrigerate and let the whey drip out for at least 4 hours or overnight, pouring some of the whey into a jar a couple of times along the way so the bowl doesn't overfill. The whey will keep in the refrigerator for about 6 months. The resulting strained yogurt will keep for about 2 weeks.

Nondairy Starter Cultures

There are a variety of lactose-free alternatives to whey that can be substituted in equal amounts. Make sure the flavor of your starter matches the flavor of your ferment—don't jump-start your applesauce with pickle juice! Saving some of the juices from the current batch of whatever you're fermenting (pickle juice from your last batch of pickles or a little reserved beet kvass for the next, for example) is a handy practice to get into. Here are a few suggestions:

Beet kvass (page 61)

Coconut water kefir (page 41)

Kimchi juice (page 25)

Kombucha (page 44)

Pickle juice (page 29)

Raw apple cider vinegar (for grains)

Water kefir (page 42)

A chinese pickling jar with chiles, garlic, and herbs fermenting in a salt brine.

CLOCKWISE FROM TOP LEFT: Yellow Beet, Beet Green, and Sichuan Peppercorn Sauerkraut; Pink Sauerkraut (with carrots); Juniper Berry, White Pepper, and Arame Sauerkraut; and Pink Sauerkraut.

SAUERKRAUT: REAL PICKLED CABBAGE

Makes 2 quarts (2 liters)

I have very few passed-down food memories, but I am certain that my Eastern European ancestors were sauerkraut eaters. That would explain both my love of kraut and my mom's and my habit of stealing a forkful straight from the jar at whim throughout the day. My favorite time to eat my sauerkraut is just after breakfast; it gets my taste buds revved up for an active day of testing and tasting in the kitchen, and when I have a hankering for something sweet but it's not yet time for dessert, a little kraut will cut through my craving and keep me eating clean through dinner. I love to cook with kraut, and I've included sauerkraut as an ingredient in recipes throughout the book.

What happens to cabbage to turn it into sauerkraut is lacto-fermentation in action: Lactic acid–producing bacteria—good guys in the world of bacteria—cause the pH of the cabbage to be lowered, making the environment unsuitable for bad bacteria (the kind that cause spoilage) and hence make the cabbage more digestible, more nutritious, and full of probiotic goodness. So to ensure successful sauerkraut making, we do all we can to encourage the good bacteria and keep the bad bacteria out. The two most important ways of achieving this are using adequate salt (that is, pure sea salt; salts containing additives can interfere with the fermentation process) and making sure your cabbage is covered in brine as it ferments. Starting with room-temperature cabbage makes pounding it easier, and note that red cabbage is drier than green cabbage, so it will need more pounding and/or brine.

Keeping these points in mind, sauerkraut is a very simple ferment to make; you can put it together with just two ingredients—cabbage and salt—though the mix-in and seasoning options are infinite and this is where you can really get creative with your kraut. You might like to start with a basic sauerkraut, experiment with one or all of my variations, and then once you're comfortable with

kraut making, go ahead and mix and match to come up with your own signature sauerkraut blends.

This recipe is for 2 quarts (2 liters) sauerkraut; if you are using a large-size crock for big-batch sauerkraut making, scale the recipe up according to the size of your vessel.

TOOLS FOR SAUERKRAUT MAKING:

- Large nonreactive bowl
- Chef's knife, food processor, mandoline, or grater
- Kitchen pounder, meat mallet, large pestle, or other kitchen instrument you can pound with
- Weight that fits in the fermentation vessel to keep the sauerkraut in its brine (drinking glass or small ramekin with a small rock for smaller vessels; plate or bowl topped with a zip-top bag filled with brine, jug filled with water, or large rock for bigger vessels)
- 2-quart (2-liter) wide-mouth jar with plastic lid or ceramic crock or food-grade plastic bucket if you are scaling up the recipe
- Clean dish towel

INGREDIENTS:

One 5-pound (2.25-kilogram) head cabbage

2 to 3 tablespoons fine sea salt

Remove the outer leaves from the cabbage. Cut the cabbage in half and remove the root end from each half (you can include the core in your sauerkraut). Chop or grate the cabbage in any thickness you like. I like a crunchy kraut, so I'll quarter my cabbage, slice it into lengthwise strips, then chop the strips. Put half the cabbage along with half the salt in a large nonreactive bowl. Massage the salt into the cabbage very well to release water from it and start to create a salty brine. To speed up the process, you can finish by pounding your cabbage with a kitchen pounder (pounding may sound intimidating, but it can be a lot of fun and it gives you the chance to pound your worries away). Repeat with the remaining cabbage and salt in the same bowl. (Or try simply mixing the cabbage with the salt and setting it aside for a few hours until it wilts.)

Pack the cabbage into a 2-quart (2-liter) jar a little at a time with at least 1 inch (2.5 centimeters) of space remaining at the top; after each addition, pound it down with your pounder to release more water. You'll know you've released enough water when the brine covers the surface of your cabbage. If it doesn't, keep pounding or add some Basic Salt Brine (page 20). Or try simply leaving it with a weight overnight and brine most likely will form.

Set up a weight for your fermentation vessel (see the choices on the previous page) to keep the cabbage covered in brine. Place the vessel on a rimmed plate (a glass pie plate works nicely) to catch any potential overflow, cover with a clean dish towel to keep out insects, and set aside in a cool place away from sunlight to ferment. Check every day to make sure the cabbage is covered with brine, pressing down on it or adding a little extra brine if it isn't. If any mold develops, remove it, clean your weight if it came into contact with the mold, and don't worry; you've created an anaerobic environment in which it is almost impossible for bad bacteria to take root. Your sauerkraut will be ready in 1 to 4 weeks, depending on the season and kitchen temperature and how tangy you like your kraut. Taste it along the way to check for doneness and consider eating from it at various stages of fermentation for some cultural diversity. Cover and place in the refrigerator, where it will keep for at least a year.

VARIATIONS

PINK SAUERKRAUT: Use half red cabbage and half green cabbage or all red cabbage. Or use green cabbage and add a shredded beet.

CUMIN SAUERKRAUT: Add 1 tablespoon toasted cumin seeds.

CARAWAY SAUERKRAUT: Add 1 tablespoon toasted caraway seeds.

KILLER CHILE SAUERKRAUT: Add a handful of dried chiles, your choice of heat level; crush them to release their seeds for extra spiciness.

JUNIPER BERRY, WHITE PEPPER, AND ARAME SAUERKRAUT: Add 1 tablespoon juniper berries, 1 tablespoon white peppercorns, and a handful of arame seaweed.

YELLOW BEET, BEET GREEN, AND SICHUAN PEPPERCORN SAUERKRAUT: Add 2 julienned yellow beets; chop the stems and greens and add them, too, along with 2 teaspoons Sichuan peppercorns.

No two batches of sauerkraut will taste exactly alike (that's one of the miracles of fermentation), and the seasonings and other ingredients you put into the jar will affect the flavor of the dishes you use them in. This gives you a chance to add a uniquely personal touch to your recipes.

Recipes starring sauerkraut:

Kale and Beet Salad (page 92)

Old-School Apple Cabbage Slaw (page 95)

Butternut Squash, Sauerkraut, and Hot Sausage Soup (page 107)

Fish Tacos with the Works (page 143)

KIMCHI: KOREAN CLASSIC KRAUT

Makes 2 quarts (2 liters)

This fermented cabbage is a national dish of Korea; it's served as a side to just about every Korean meal and it makes its way into soups, stews, pancakes, and any number of main-dish recipes in that country's cuisine and in this book. There are many different styles of kimchi; what most have in common is that they call for first soaking cabbage in brine before fermenting and they typically include hot pepper, ginger, garlic, fish or anchovy sauce, and dried shrimp. I've included an option for making it vegetarian by swapping in another ferment, miso, and omitting the dried shrimp. The most common base is Napa cabbage and daikon radish, but variations abound.

If this recipe whets your appetite, you might want to look at Lauryn Chun's *The Kimchi Cookbook,* which offers sixty different seasonal kimchi variations. If you like a super-crisp kimchi, use just the stalks of the cabbage, increasing the amount of stalks to equal 2 pounds (900 grams), and set aside the tender top parts for salads or stir-fries. Korean red pepper powder, fish sauce, and salted shrimp (also fermented) can be found in Korean and Asian markets. Make sure your fish sauce doesn't contain additives or preservatives, as these could inhibit fermentation. Red Boat is a new artisanal brand that boasts all-natural, extra-virgin first-press processing.

TOOLS FOR KIMCHI MAKING:

- Large nonreactive bowl
- Plate or bowl that fits in the bowl to keep the cabbage in its brine
- Weight that fits in the fermentation vessel to keep the kimchi in its brine (drinking glass or small ramekin with a small rock for smaller vessels; plate or bowl topped with a zip-top bag filled with brine, jug filled with water, or large rock for bigger vessels)
- 2-quart (2-liter) wide-mouth jar or ceramic crock or food-grade plastic bucket if you are scaling up the recipe
- Clean dish towel

INGREDIENTS:

One 2½-pound (1.2-kilogram) head Napa cabbage

About 2 quarts (2 liters) Basic Salt Brine (page 20)

1 small daikon radish (about 10 ounces/285 grams), peeled and cut into 2-inch (5-centimeter) matchsticks

2 large carrots, peeled and cut into 2-inch (5-centimeter) matchsticks

5 scallions, white and green parts, cut into 1-inch (2.5-centimeter) pieces

2 teaspoons Korean salted shrimp, minced (optional; omit for vegetarians)

1 to 8 tablespoons Korean red pepper powder

¼ cup (60 milliliters) fish sauce, or 2 tablespoons light miso paste dissolved in ¼ cup (60 milliliters) water

2 tablespoons grated fresh unpeeled ginger

6 large garlic cloves, minced

Cut the cabbage in half lengthwise, then into quarters; core it and separate it into individual leaves. Fill a large nonreactive bowl with water and swish the leaves around in the water to clean them. Rinse the bowl.

Cut the cabbage leaves crosswise into 2-inch (5-centimeter) pieces. Put them in the bowl and add enough brine to just cover, making sure the cabbage is submerged. Place a plate over the cabbage and top it with a heavy weight such as a zip-top bag filled with brine (so that if it accidentally breaks, brine rather than water goes into the jar), a jug filled with water, or a rock.

Cover with a clean dish towel and set aside for at least 2 hours and up to 24 hours, pressing on the weight from time to time to make sure the cabbage stays submerged in the brine. Drain in a colander, reserving the brine. Gently squeeze out the excess liquid and return the cabbage to the bowl. Add the daikon, carrots, scallions, and salted shrimp, if using.

In a medium bowl, combine the red pepper powder, fish sauce, ginger, and garlic and stir to form a paste. Add the paste to the cabbage mixture; put on disposable gloves and use your hands to thoroughly coat the vegetables with the paste. Pack the mixture along with its juices tightly into a clean 2-quart (2-liter) glass jar (if there is extra, pack it into a smaller jar); press on it to release liquid and form a brine. If the cabbage is not completely covered in brine, add some reserved brine.

Set up a weight for your fermentation vessel (see the choices above) to keep the kimchi covered in brine. Place the vessel on a rimmed plate (a glass pie plate works nicely) to catch any potential overflow, cover with a clean dish towel to keep out insects, and set aside in a cool place away from sunlight to ferment. Check every day to make sure the cabbage is covered with brine, pressing down on it or adding a little extra brine if it isn't. If any mold develops, remove it, clean your weight if it came into contact with the mold, and don't worry; you've created an anaerobic environment in which it is almost impossible for bad bacteria to take root. Your kimchi will be ready in 3 days to 2 weeks, depending on the season and kitchen temperature and how tangy you like it. Taste it along the way to check for doneness and consider eating from it at various stages of fermentation for some cultural diversity. Cover and place in the refrigerator, where it will keep for about 6 months.

VARIATIONS

BOK CHOY KIMCHI: Substitute 3 pounds (1.4 kilograms) whole baby bok choy leaves for the Napa cabbage.

BRUSSELS SPROUTS KIMCHI: Substitute 2 pounds (900 grams) Brussels sprouts, trimmed and cut in half, for the Napa cabbage.

Recipes starring kimchi:

Devil's Fried Eggs with Bacon and Kimchi (page 52)

Pickle Mary (page 63)

Kimchi, Scallion, and Toasted Sesame Oil Dressing (page 89)

Cheesy Kimchi Pancakes (page 122)

Hot and Sweet Wings with Creamy Gorgonzola Dressing (page 128)

Fish Tacos with the Works (page 143)

Korean-Style Rice Bowl with Kimchi (page 146)

Crunchy Kimchi Pork (page 149)

Kimchi Juice as Health Tonic

Kimchi is packed with vitamins and minerals, and the brine formed from making it can be decanted and served in shot glasses as an energy or cold-prevention tonic. Fermented cabbage is also high in vitamin C and minerals and has been shown to have cancer-preventive properties, making kimchi an important part of your fermentation rotation.

FROM TOP: Kimchi, Brussels Sprouts Kimchi, and Bok Choy Kimchi.

CUCUMBER PICKLES: DILL AND BEYOND

Makes 2 quarts (2 liters)

If you are new to fermentation, there's no better place to start than with pickles. Just about everyone knows and loves them, and they are truly easy to make. All that's required is a jar, cucumbers, salt, and seasonings, and a little patience as you wait for the salty-sour transformation of cucumber to pickle. Making pickles is reason enough for starting a fermentation habit, as the taste of salt-brined pickles is more complex than shelf-stable, store-bought vinegar pickles, which contain no active cultures. This is one of the sad side effects of an industrialized food system; through big-batch standardization, a living food that played an important part of Old World food culture turned into a processed food. Let's make a batch of real pickles and reclaim tradition!

This recipe is for the standard dill, with variations opposite. If you are lucky enough to have access to grape leaves, currant leaves, or horseradish leaves, add a couple to your pickle jar, as I've been told they help to keep the pickles crisp. This recipe is for 2 quarts (2 liters) pickles; if you are using a large-size crock for big-batch pickle making, scale the recipe up according to the size of your vessel.

TOOLS FOR CUCUMBER PICKLE MAKING:

- 2-quart (2-liter) wide-mouth jar or ceramic crock or food-grade plastic bucket if you are scaling up the recipe

- Weight that fits in the fermentation vessel to keep the pickles in their brine (drinking glass or small ramekin with a small rock for smaller vessels; plate or bowl topped with a zip-top bag filled with brine, jug filled with water, or large rock for bigger vessels)

- Clean dish towel

INGREDIENTS:

2 large handfuls fresh dill fronds, or 1 tablespoon dried dill seeds

5 small garlic cloves, peeled

1 teaspoon whole black peppercorns

2 pounds (950 grams) small to medium kirby or pickling cucumbers, rinsed

About 3 cups (720 milliliters) Basic Salt Brine (page 20)

Put the dill, garlic, and peppercorns in a 2-quart (2-liter) jar or pickling crock, then put the cucumbers on top. Pour enough brine over the cucumbers to cover them, leaving at least 1 inch (2.5 centimeters) of space remaining at the top.

Set up a weight for your fermentation vessel (see the choices at left). Place the jar on a rimmed plate (a glass pie plate works nicely) to catch any potential overflow, cover with a clean dish towel to keep out insects, and set aside in a cool place away from sunlight to ferment. Check your soon-to-be pickles every day and remove mold if any develops (don't worry if you don't get all of the mold; you've created an anaerobic environment in which it is virtually impossible for bad bacteria to take root). Bubbles may start to rise and the brine will become cloudy; this is a sign of healthy fermentation. Your pickles will be ready in 1 to 2 weeks, depending on the season and kitchen temperature and whether you like them half sour or fully sour. Cover and place in the refrigerator, where they will keep for about 2 months. As cucumbers have a soft cell wall, they start to get mushy sooner than firmer ferments such as sauerkraut and root vegetables; when that happens it's time to make soup (page 110 or 112).

VARIATIONS

HORSERADISH AND GINGER CUCUMBER PICKLES: Instead of the dill, garlic, and peppercorns, add 1 ounce (25 grams/about 6 tablespoons) finely grated fresh horseradish and 1 finely grated 2-inch (5-centimeter) piece unpeeled ginger (the peel contains its own good bacteria) to the jar before you add the cucumbers. After brining, cover and shake to distribute the seasonings and give it another shake every time you grab a pickle from the jar. They will get more infused with flavor the longer they sit.

CORIANDER AND CILANTRO CUCUMBER PICKLES: Instead of the dill, add an equal amount of fresh cilantro and 2 tablespoons coriander seeds.

CINNAMON AND RED CHILE PICKLES: Instead of the dill, garlic, and peppercorns, add 3 cinnamon sticks and 3 dried red chiles.

DILLY BEANS: Substitute 1 pound (450 grams) trimmed green beans for the cucumbers, include both the fresh dill and dried dill, and add 1 tablespoon Live and Kickin' Hot Sauce (page 81) or 1 tablespoon red chile flakes.

GREEN CHILE AND MINT PICKLES: Instead of the dill and peppercorns, add 2 large handfuls of fresh mint with their stems and a handful or so of fresh green chiles.

PLAIN CUCUMBER PICKLES: Use just pickles and salt; the pure salt highlights the natural flavor of the cucumbers.

YOUNG ZUCCHINI PICKLES: Substitute small seasonal zucchini, pattypan, or yellow squash for the cucumbers.

LIVE AND KICKIN' PICKLED PEPPERS: Ferment whole chiles in brine using the cucumber pickle–making method on page 28, adding your choice of herbs and seasonings, or pickle them plain for a pure hit of heat.

Recipes starring cucumber pickles:
Pickle Mary (page 63)
Poseidon Salad (page 96)
Pickle Salad Two Ways (page 101)
Polish-Style Cold Beet Soup (page 110)

Pickle Juice

After you're done with your pickles, you'll have plenty of brine left over. Keep it, as you can use it in many ways: in dressing, as a marinade ingredient to tenderize meat, to flavor soups or sauces, or to sip after a meal to help with digestion. You can also use it as a starter instead of salt or whey as you're making other ferments; if you plan to do so, reach into the pickle jar with a fork rather than your hands as you enjoy your batches to avoid introducing potentially unfriendly bacteria into the pickle juice.

Pickled carrots and parsnips with tumeric and black mustard seeds.

ROOT VEGETABLES:
PERFECT PRESERVATIONISTS

Hearty and strong roots take well to fermentation, and they can be cultured in both the brining method (as for cucumber pickles) and the pounding method (as for sauerkraut).

For the brining method, vegetable sticks are soaked in salt brine; for the pounding method, they are grated and pounded in salt. We'll use carrots here as our example, but the method works for beets, parsnips, kohlrabi, burdock, daikon, rutabaga, turnips, and other sturdy root vegetables as well (note that yields will vary from root to root as they are grated, so you may need to adjust the amount up or down a little to fill the jar; keep the amount of salt the same). Root vegetable sticks make for great snacking, are perfect served on a crudité or antipasto platter, and when chopped they make a flavorful addition to salads and sandwiches or a garnish to any number of soups or entrées. Grated root vegetables can be served as a condiment or mixed with fresh ingredients such as in Carrot and Arame Salad (page 33).

Brining Method for Pickling Carrots
(or other root vegetables)
Makes 2 pints (2 half-liters)

TOOLS FOR ROOT VEGETABLE PICKLE MAKING (BRINE METHOD):

• Two 1-pint (half-liter) wide-mouth jars

• Clean dish towel

INGREDIENTS:

Herbs and spices: 4 to 6 thyme or rosemary sprigs, 4 bay leaves, handful of dried chiles or whole black peppercorns, and any flavors of your imagination

About 1½ pounds (680 grams) scrubbed carrots, cut into crudité-size sticks the length of the jar (for small carrots, you can leave them whole and ferment them longer)

About 2 cups (480 milliliters) Basic Salt Brine (page 20)

Put the herbs and/or spices in two 1-pint (half-liter) jars; turn the jars on their sides and, working horizontally, tightly pack the carrots into the jars (the carrots will shrink a little as they ferment; packing them tightly prevents them from floating as they shrink). Pour enough brine over the carrots to cover them, leaving at least 1 inch (2.5 centimeters) of space remaining at the top. If the carrots float in the brine, wedge in another carrot stick or two. Cover with a lid or airlock (page 19).

Place the jars on a rimmed plate (a glass pie plate works nicely) to catch any potential leakage or bubbling over when you open the lid, cover with a clean dish towel to keep out insects, and set aside in a cool place away from sunlight to ferment. After a few days, check your carrots, removing mold if any develops (don't worry if you don't get all of the mold; you've created an anaerobic environment in which it is almost impossible for bad bacteria to take root). The brine may start to look a little cloudy, and bubbly froth will form at the top. You'll also see bubbles forming in the carrots at the top, which is a normal sign of fermentation. When you check your carrots, occasionally taste one to see how far they've fermented and decide if they have soured to your liking. Your carrots will be ready in 3 days to 2 weeks, depending on the season and kitchen temperature and how tangy and crunchy you like them. Place in the refrigerator, covered, where they will keep for about 6 months.

Pounding Method for Pickling Carrots
(or other root vegetables)
Makes 1 quart (1 liter)

TOOLS FOR ROOT VEGETABLE PICKLE MAKING (POUNDING METHOD):

• Large nonreactive bowl

• Food processor or grater

• Kitchen pounder, meat mallet, large pestle, or other kitchen instrument you can pound with

• 1-quart (1-liter) wide-mouth jar

• Drinking glass or small ramekin with a rock to weight it that fits in the fermentation vessel to keep the vegetables submerged

• Clean dish towel

INGREDIENTS:

1¾ pounds (790 grams) carrots, scrubbed, ends trimmed, and coarsely grated (about 4 cups packed grated carrots)

1 teaspoon fine sea salt

Seasonings: grated or sliced fresh unpeeled ginger or turmeric, garlic, dried chiles, mustard seeds, cumin seeds, and any flavors of your imagination

Basic Salt Brine (page 20), if needed

Put the carrots and salt in a large nonreactive bowl. Massage the salt into the carrots very well to release water from them and start to create a salty brine. Then begin pounding with a kitchen pounder to release more brine; this will take about 3 minutes. Add your seasonings.

Pack the carrots into the jar a little at a time; after each addition pound with your pounder to release more water. You'll know you've released enough when the brine covers the surface of your carrots. If it doesn't, keep pounding or add brine.

Place a glass filled with water or a small ramekin with a rock placed in it that fits snugly into your jar and press down on it until the brine rises over the level of the carrots, leaving at least 1 inch (2.5 centimeters) of space remaining at the top.

Place the jar on a rimmed plate (a glass pie plate works nicely) to catch any potential overflow, cover with a clean dish towel to keep out insects, and set aside in a cool place away from sunlight to ferment. Check every day to make sure the carrots are covered with brine, pressing down on them or adding a little brine if they aren't. If any mold develops, remove it, and don't worry; you've created an anaerobic environment in which it is almost impossible for bad bacteria to take root. Your carrots will be ready in 1 to 2 weeks, depending on the season and kitchen temperature and how tangy and crunchy you like them. Taste along the way to check for doneness and consider eating from various stages of fermentation for some cultural diversity. Cover and place in the refrigerator, where the carrots will keep for about 6 months.

A few flavoring suggestions:

Carrots with grated fresh ginger

Parsnips with grated fresh turmeric and mustard seeds

Rutabaga with ground cloves and cardamom

Beets with caraway

Turnips with cumin and dill seeds

Recipes starring pickled root vegetables:

Carrot and Arame Salad (opposite)

Sushi Bar–Style Salad (page 91)

Collard Green Wrap with Creamy Cashew Cheese and Sweet Mango Chutney (page 135)

(And look for them as a "Swap" for fresh vegetables in recipes throughout the book.)

CARROT AND ARAME SALAD
Makes about 3 cups (500 grams)

Pickled root vegetables are great straight up as a side or snack to munch on, or can be mixed and matched with fresh vegetables, cooked vegetables, or a variety of sea vegetables, as in this simple recipe that was born out of a batch of too-salty pickled carrots. Instead of composting the whole batch, I looked for something to cut the salt: Mixing the carrots with arame, a seaweed loaded with trace minerals, was my simple and flavorful solution.

1 cup (15 grams) arame seaweed, soaked in water to cover for 20 minutes

1 cup (300 grams) shredded pickled carrots (opposite; try flavoring them with ginger)

Fresh lemon juice (optional)

Extra-virgin olive oil

Toasted sesame seeds (optional)

Drain the seaweed soaking water (see Tip). Return the arame to the bowl and stir in the carrots. Add a splash of lemon juice if you like. Serve drizzled with oil and toasted sesame seeds, if using.

SWAP: Substitute shredded pickled turnips or parsnips for the carrots.

SUPERCHARGE: Top with a dollop of Greek yogurt (page 37) or Countertop Crème Fraîche (page 79).

SHORTCUT: Use store-bought shredded pickled carrots, making sure the jar comes from the refrigerator case and is marked *raw, unpasteurized,* or *naturally fermented.*

TIP: Water your plants with the arame soaking water.

Sixties Counterculture: I'll Pass on the Twinkies, but Please Pass the Kraut!

Whole Foods Encyclopedia author Rebecca Wood, who in the 1960s studied in Boston with preeminent macrobiotics teacher Michio Kushi, recounts that eating brown rice and fermenting cabbage were as much a part of being counterculture as were tie-dye shirts and bell-bottom pants.

As part of the burgeoning natural foods movement, Kushi helped popularize fermentation and made available for the first time foods like brown rice, miso, tamari, and tempeh. By the 1970s, major urban centers were offering macrobiotic cooking classes where people learned, among other things, to make sauerkraut and dill pickles and to bring traditional foods back into their diets. In the 1970s and '80s William Shurtleff contributed to the movement with his seminal books on tofu, tempeh, and miso, which continue to be in print today. Says Rebecca, "On principle we passed on Twinkies, but please pass the kraut!"

YOGURT: A MOST FAMILIAR FERMENT, WITH UNFAMILIAR FORAYS

Makes 2 quarts (2 liters)

Yogurt is an everyday ferment for many people, the one we most associate with probiotics and good health. Here you'll learn how to make your own dairy yogurt with an option for turning it into Greek yogurt. Two dairy-free alternatives—young coconut yogurt and almond milk yogurt—are also included. Enjoy your yogurt by the bowlful or take it further and put it to use in any of the book's sweet or savory recipes that feature it as an ingredient.

Dairy yogurt is by far the most familiar ferment in this book, with whole supermarket refrigerator cases dedicated to this cultured milk product, some probiotic-rich brands and many others filled with sugar, additives, and thickeners and lacking in the very live cultures that made it famous. Make your own and your perception of yogurt will be forever changed. If you'd like your yogurt to be completely live, start with raw milk and heat it to a lower temperature (110°F/43°C) than you would for pasteurized milk; the rest of the yogurt-making instructions are the same. Your homemade yogurt, particularly raw milk yogurt, will likely be thinner and tangier than store-bought; strain it and you'll have rich, thick, and slightly sweet Greek yogurt (see page 37). Note that plain, whole milk yogurt is assumed for all recipes that call for dairy yogurt.

TOOLS FOR YOGURT MAKING:

• Large saucepan

• Candy thermometer

INGREDIENTS:

Two 1-quart (1-liter) glass jars plus one 1-pint (½-liter) jar

2 quarts (2 liters) organic raw or pasteurized whole milk (see Live Yogurt Start to Finish, page 36)

½ cup (120 milliliters) organic whole milk plain yogurt with active cultures and no additives or thickeners, or an heirloom starter culture (see Resources, page 183)

Pour the milk into a large saucepan and attach a candy thermometer to the side of it. Gently heat the milk over medium heat, stirring often to prevent scorching the bottom of the pan, until the milk reaches 180°F (82°C) for pasteurized milk or 110°F (43°C) if you're starting with raw milk and wish to make raw milk yogurt. Turn off the heat and pasteurized milk let cool to 110°F (43°C); raw milk is ready to go.

Stir the yogurt or starter culture into the milk to dissolve it. Pour the milk into the glass jars and cover each. Place the jars in a warm place where the temperature will remain around 110°F (43°C). Options include a yogurt maker, an oven that has a pilot light, a food dehydrator with removable shelves, or a cooler that you fill with hot water up to the necks of the jars (remove the towel first); alternatively, you can put the milk mixture in a Thermos that retains its heat well instead of the jars, or wrap the jars with heating pads. Leave undisturbed for at least 8 hours or up to 24 hours for a full fermentation (see Full Fermentation on page 36). Let cool completely, then refrigerate until ready to eat. Save some yogurt as a starter for your next batch. If you are using store-bought yogurt as your starter, you will need a new starter every several batches; an heirloom starter culture can last indefinitely. Taking a bit of your just-made yogurt and immediately freezing it (when it's at its point of perfection) ensures a vibrant starter for your next batch.

CLOCKWISE FROM TOP LEFT: dairy yogurt, dairy kefir (page 39), Coconut Kefir Cream (page 165), Greek yogurt (page 37), and Young Coconut Yogurt (page 37).

Recipes starring yogurt:

Turkish-Style Poached Eggs with Garlicky Yogurt and Smoky Butter (page 54)

Sweet or Salty Lassi (page 69)

Chai Spice Yogurt Latte (page 57)

Summer Chowder (page 112)

Polish-Style Cold Beet Soup (page 110)

Mexican Charred Corn with Greek Yogurt and Salted Plum Vinegar (page 127)

Moroccan-Style Lamb Stew with Prunes and Preserved Lemon (page 156)

Greek-Style Turkey Meatballs with Tzatziki Sauce (page 141)

Real-Deal Blueberry Frozen Yogurt (page 173)

Devilish Cupcakes (page 178)

Full Fermentation

Commercial yogurt is often fermented for very short amounts of time; thickening agents sometimes are added as a shortcut to give it the thick and creamy texture we associate with good yogurt. Another insult to this once living food is double pasteurization: Pasteurized milk is fermented with live active cultures and then pasteurized again, so we're left with no active cultures. The best way to know if this is the case with any particular brand is to check with the manufacturer.

A full fermentation of twenty-four hours ensures that most or all of the lactose has been eaten by the good bacteria (which is why some lactose-intolerant people are able to eat yogurt) and the probiotic cultures are at full force, supercharged to keep our gut flora balanced, just what we expect from real yogurt.

Live Yogurt Start to Finish

When we talk about the traditional foods our ancestors ate, raw milk was as standard as cultured foods like sauerkraut and pickles. Heating milk to high temperatures—pasteurization—was something that came along during our changeover to a less localized food system when food was going places and dependable refrigeration was not yet in place. Today good raw milk can be bought from a farmer or retailer you trust; this milk is full of enzymes and good bacteria, making it a natural base for yogurt that is live from start to finish. (Some populations that traditionally start with raw milk heat the milk to higher temperatures than start-to-finish live yogurt to give the yogurt more body, but heating milk at home for yogurt making doesn't have the same effect as full-fledged pasturization.)

Laws for buying raw milk vary by state; a few don't allow it, some permit it to be sold freely in stores, and some require that you buy it at the farm. The latter is the case for my state of Vermont; talking to the farmers gives me confidence in the products they sell. For a state-by-state guide, go to Raw Milk Nation (www.farmtoconsumer.org). Raw milk is not a choice everyone feels comfortable with; if pasteurized is your comfort zone, know that your homemade yogurt will still be brimming with beneficial bacteria!

Homemade Buttermilk

It's hard to get a good old-fashioned glass of buttermilk (traditionally made as a byproduct of the buttermaking process). You can make your own real buttermilk containing live cultures quite simply: Stir ¼ cup (60 milliliters) commercial buttermilk or ¼ cup (60 milliliters) yogurt or whey (page 20) into 1 cup (240 milliliters) whole milk, cover loosely, and let sit in a warm place for up to 2 days, until thickened and sour to your liking. You can repeat this several times before the culture loses its strength. To keep your buttermilk going indefinitely, purchasing a reusable buttermilk starter (see Resources, page 183) is the way to go.

GREEK YOGURT

Makes about 2 cups (480 milliliters) yogurt,
plus 2 cups (480 milliliters) whey

Greek yogurt, also known as strained yogurt, yogurt cheese, or *labneh*, is simply yogurt that's been strained to concentrate it, with the whey (the liquid part) separated out. The whey can be saved and used as a fermentation starter (see page 19).

Greek yogurt is all the rage in stores, but be careful what you buy: True Greek yogurt is made from the same ingredients as yogurt—milk and a starter. Skip store-bought brands that contain thickeners to imitate true Greek yogurt. Greek yogurt has less sugar and fewer carbohydrates than regular yogurt and is less tangy, with a lovely creaminess that works well in recipes: When whisked into a sauce or soup, it doesn't curdle as readily as regular yogurt can. If you use sheep's-milk yogurt (as is traditional in Greece), it will be the creamiest ever.

TOOLS FOR GREEK YOGURT MAKING:

• Strainer and double layer of cheesecloth

• Large bowl

INGREDIENT:

1 quart (1 liter) whole milk yogurt, homemade
   (see page 34) or store-bought

Line a strainer with a double layer of cheesecloth or a new handkerchief (a double layer of paper towels can work in a pinch). Place it atop a bowl and pour the yogurt into the strainer. Cover with a dish towel and set aside in the refrigerator for at least 4 hours or overnight. (Strain it for longer, about 24 hours, perhaps adding herbs to infuse it with flavor, and you have yogurt cheese, delicious as a cream cheese–like spread or dip, or rolled into balls, placed in a jar, and marinated in olive oil.) Remove from the strainer, spoon the yogurt into a jar, and refrigerate; pour the whey into a separate jar, refrigerate, and save it as a fermentation starter.

YOUNG COCONUT YOGURT

Makes about 28 ounces (790 grams)

Yogurt made from young coconuts is divinely rich, full of healthy fats, and a great yogurt alternative for those who are dairy free. Young coconuts are soft, off-white, with pointed tops, unlike the more commonly recognizable dark brown, hard-shelled, hairy mature coconuts.

For this recipe you could buy several fresh coconuts, crack them, and scoop the flesh from the shells, but most of us don't have that kind of time, so this recipe uses frozen young coconut meat and water, which you can find in some natural food stores and Asian food stores (made sure the brand you choose contains no sugar) and online. Choose raw, unpasteurized coconut water from the refrigerator or freezer section rather than the pasteurized kind often found in boxes or cans. You'll need nondairy yogurt starter for this yogurt.

TOOLS FOR YOUNG COCONUT YOGURT MAKING:

• Blender, preferably a high-speed one

• Yogurt maker or a dehydrator with removable shelves
  and small nonreactive jars with lids

INGREDIENTS:

One 16-ounce (454-gram) package frozen young coconut
   meat (see Resources, page 183)

12 ounces (354 milliliters) raw young coconut water, fresh
   or frozen

1/4 teaspoon nondairy yogurt starter culture (see
   Resources, page 183)

Defrost the coconut meat and coconut water in the refrigerator if it was frozen; this will take between 36 and 48 hours (to fast-track defrosting, place the sealed containers in a bowl in the sink and run it under a constant stream of cold water from the tap for a few minutes). Combine the coconut meat and coconut water in a blender (a high-speed blender yields the creamiest results, but a regular blender will work too;

increase the blending time a little) and blend, starting on low speed and gradually increasing the speed to high; blend on high speed for 3 minutes, stopping the machine a couple of times so the coconut doesn't get overheated. Add the starter culture and blend on high speed for another 2 minutes, again stopping the machine a couple of times so the coconut doesn't get overheated (heating it above 115°F/46°C can kill the culture).

Pour into your yogurt maker's cups with the lids off, place in the yogurt maker, and leave to incubate for 12 hours. Alternatively, pour the yogurt into jars, place the jars in a dehydrator with removable shelves, set the machine to 110°F (43°C), and leave it for 12 hours to set. Remove from the machine, put the lids on the cups, and cool for 30 minutes. Transfer to the refrigerator and leave for 24 hours before serving. The yogurt will keep for up to 2 weeks in the refrigerator.

ALMOND MILK YOGURT
Makes 42 ounces (1.25 liters)

Here's a second dairy-free yogurt, perfect as a drinking yogurt, as it produces a lot of whey; it separates with the solid layer floating on top. Stir it and sip it straight from the jar, or strain it through cheesecloth or a nut milk bag for about an hour for a deliciously creamy and thick Greek-style almond yogurt (but be aware that you'll end up with less than a third of the batch).

TOOLS FOR ALMOND MILK YOGURT MAKING:

• Yogurt maker or a dehydrator with removable shelves and small nonreactive jars with lids

INGREDIENTS:

¼ teaspoon nondairy yogurt starter culture (see Resources, page 183)

3 cups (720 milliliters) almond milk (opposite)

Whisk the starter culture into the almond milk. Pour into your yogurt maker's cups with the lids off, place in the yogurt maker, and leave to incubate for 10 to 12 hours. Alternatively, pour the yogurt into jars, place the jars in a dehydrator with removable shelves, set the machine to 110°F (43°C), and leave it for 10 to 12 hours to set. Remove from the machine, put the lids on the cups, and cool for 30 minutes. Transfer to the refrigerator and leave for 24 hours before serving. The yogurt will keep for up to 2 weeks in the refrigerator.

Almond Milk
Makes about 1 quart (1 liter)

1½ cups (225 grams) almonds (see Note)

4 cups (1 liter) filtered water

Put the almonds in a glass measuring cup and rinse them until the water runs clear. In a medium bowl, soak the almonds in filtered water to cover by a couple of inches for at least 12 hours or up to 24 hours. Drain and rinse the almonds well, put them in the blender, and add the filtered water. Blend at high speed until smooth; this will take about 2 minutes. Strain through a nut milk bag or strainer lined with cheesecloth into a bowl; squeeze on the pulp to extract all the liquid.

Pour into a bottle and refrigerate until ready to use; it will keep refrigerated for up to 4 days. Cashews or Brazil nuts could be substituted for the almonds (reduce the soaking time to 4 hours).

NOTE: If you'd like to make almond cheese with the leftover almond pulp (see page 84), peel your almonds before blending them: Place a soaked almond between your forefinger and thumb, squeeze, and the peel should pop right off (if it doesn't, pour some hot water over the almonds and try again).

SHORTCUT: Strain your almond milk by pressing it through a French press instead of a nut milk bag. This efficient method saves on cleanup time; make sure to wash your press well first to remove any coffee residue or use a dedicated press for your almond-milk making.

KEFIR:
THE "FEEL-GOOD" CULTURED MILK DRINK

Makes 1 quart (1 liter)

Kefir, a probiotic beverage made by adding kefir grains to liquid, traditionally milk, was one of the first ferments to come out of my kitchen as I began to dabble in the craft of culturing. This tangy and slightly effervescent cultured milk beverage is often referred to as a drinkable yogurt. Yogurt *plus* might be a more accurate description, as kefir contains a greater variety of strains of probiotics and beneficial yeasts than yogurt, and the probiotics in kefir work to directly colonize your gut. The Turkish translation of *kefir*, "to feel good," is a fitting description.

Kefir originated in the Caucasus mountains centuries ago, and some say it's kefir rather than yogurt that's responsible for the longevity of these people. This superdrink has recently made its way into natural food stores, and it's catching on in a big way. As with dairy yogurt, there is little or no lactose remaining in dairy kefir, making it an option for some lactose-intolerant people. For completely dairy-free kefir, make it with coconut milk, coconut water, or almond milk. Water kefir, which uses a completely different starter (see page 42), is another nondairy kefir option (and you can also use the Water Kefir grains or some finished Water Kefir to culture your nondairy milk).

Kefir is the base for some of my favorite frozen desserts (pages 174 to 176), I use it to make a spreadable cheese, and a glass of kefir straight up makes an energizing between-meal snack.

Kefir requires a kefir starter, also referred to as kefir grains or kefir culture, which you'll reuse with each batch (see opposite on the difference between kefir grains and powdered starter). With proper upkeep, the grains can last indefinitely, and they multiply, so you can share them with friends and family. Note that plain, whole milk kefir is assumed for all recipes that call for dairy kefir.

Kefir Grains Versus Powdered Starter

The traditional way of culturing milk into kefir is with a starter in the form of a kefir culture, also known as kefir grains. They aren't made of actual grains but rather a combination of yeast and bacteria, and they look like tiny heads of cauliflower. These grains are strained from every batch and can be used over and over again to keep you flush with kefir for a lifetime.

Powdered kefir starters are a recent popular option, marketed for convenience as they are added directly to the milk, stirred, left to sit, and the kefir is ready for drinking, no straining or extra jars required. They may be a good choice for occasional kefir drinkers, but the downside is that they contain far fewer strains of bacteria, so you're getting fewer of the incredible benefits kefir has to offer. And because they are less potent, they last for only a few rounds and then you have to buy more.

I like the independence traditional fermentation affords and the community of sharing that it fosters, so I'll stick to my kefir grains. Next time you're in southern Vermont, stop by and I'll set you up with a jar!

• 1-quart (1-liter) wide-mouth jar or pitcher

• Mesh strainer

INGREDIENTS:

4 cups (1 liter) raw or pasteurized organic whole milk (see Live Yogurt Start to Finish, page 36)

About 1 tablespoon kefir starter (see Resources, page 183), more if you'd like your kefir tangier

Pour the milk into a wide-mouth jar or pitcher. Add the kefir starter. Cover the jar with a clean dish towel or cloth napkin and secure it with a rubber band. Leave at room temperature away from sunlight for 12 to 48 hours, depending on the season and kitchen temperature, until thickened and tangy to your liking.

Strain your kefir into another jar, stirring with a spoon to extract all the liquid. Cover and place your finished kefir in the refrigerator, where it will keep for several weeks. Take the grains left in the strainer, put them in a new jar of milk (no need to rinse them first), and make another batch of kefir in the same way. If you aren't ready to make another batch of fresh kefir, store the grains covered in milk in a small jar in the refrigerator for up to a week; change the milk once every week or two until you're ready to start making kefir again. Note that if a batch of kefir goes off, toss the liquid but keep the kefir grains; rinse them and they'll be good to go again.

SHORTCUT: Instead of the kefir grains, add a small amount of finished kefir to your milk. It will act as your starter without the extra step of straining; you can repeat this several times before the culture weakens and then go back to culturing with a starter. This kefir-without-cleanup method is a good option for when you're traveling.

Recipes starring kefir:

Buckwheat Pancakes (page 56)

Bibb Lettuce Salad with Creamy Gorgonzola Dressing (page 90)

Cauliflower and Raisin Salad with Saffron-Scented Lemon Dressing (page 99)

Strawberry and Cointreau Ice Cream (page 168)

Tangy Coconut Sorbet (page 174)

Raspberry-Lime Granita (page 176)

KEFIR CREAM CHEESE
Makes about 1½ cups (360 milliliters)

This tangy, spreadable cheese is made by straining kefir, similar to the method for making Greek yogurt or yogurt cheese (page 37), but you'll need to start just after completing your kefir, because in order for it to set properly it is left on the counter until the curds separate from the whey before straining; this separation cannot happen once the kefir has been refrigerated. You'll be left with a good amount of whey with every batch of cream cheese, which can be used in any recipe that calls for a starter.

4 cups (1 liter) just-made kefir (do not refrigerate before using)

Take your just-made kefir and leave it on the counter loosely covered with a clean dish towel for about 4 hours, until the curds separate from the whey .

Line a strainer with a double layer of cheesecloth. Place the strainer over a bowl and pour the curds and whey through the strainer. The curds will remain in the strainer and the whey will drip into the bowl. After about 5 minutes, pour the whey from the bowl into a jar, cover, and refrigerate it. Place the strainer and bowl in the refrigerator and let it drain for about 4 more hours or overnight. Gather the cheesecloth and squeeze it a little to get the last of the whey out; pour the additional whey into the jar you set up earlier and save it to use as a fermentation starter for another recipe. Store the kefir cheese in a covered container in the refrigerator, where it will keep for up to 1 week.

NONDAIRY KEFIR OPTIONS:
COCONUT WATER KEFIR, COCONUT MILK KEFIR, AND ALMOND MILK KEFIR

Make your kefir using the instructions on page 40, substituting an equal amount of coconut water, coconut milk from the can (use two 14-ounce/400-milliliter cans), or almond milk (page 38). Coconut Kefir Cream, made from just the cream part of the coconut milk can (page 165), makes a slightly tangy, supremely rich dessert topping. Here are some tips for nondairy kefir making:

• The standard dairy kefir starter works well for your nondairy kefir, but purists might not wish to use it because it's based on dairy. An alternative is to add ½ cup (120 milliliters) Water Kefir (the finished Water Kefir, not the grains; see page 42) to your 4 cups (1 liter) liquid (for coconut milk use two 14-ounce/400-milliliter cans and proceed with the recipe; the Water Kefir will act as your starter.

• Whisk coconut milk until smooth before adding kefir grains to make it easier to strain out the grains.

• Your dairy kefir grains can be used repeatedly for nondairy kefir, but they will not multiply. To preserve their longevity, culture them in dairy milk for 24 hours every few batches to revitalize them.

• Coconut Water Kefir also can be used as a starter to make coconut milk or almond milk kefir: add ¼ cup (60 milliliters) for each can of coconut milk or 2 cups (480 milliliters) almond milk.

• Heating coconut water, coconut milk, or almond milk gently to 90°F (32°C) before adding the kefir grains can help to jump-start fermentation (higher temperatures will compromise the grains). A shortcut is to pour boiling water into a jar, pour the water out, let cool briefly, then add the coconut water.

• Avoid coconut milk and almond milk that contain additives or sweeteners.

• Coconut milk kefir is extremely rich (perfect for coconut sorbet); dilute it with water if you're drinking it straight or adding it to a smoothie.

• Almond milk will culture quicker than other milks, normally in less than 12 hours. It will be thinner than dairy or coconut milk kefir and it will separate; give it a good shake before drinking.

WATER KEFIR

Makes 1 quart (1 liter)

Water kefir grains are sugar addicts; they live on sugar water in the same way dairy kefir grains feed on lactose. And as with the lactose in dairy kefir, the sugar is mostly or completely gone in the final Water Kefir beverage. These grains grow like crazy, allowing you to make more and more batches and to share them liberally.

Water kefir acts as a nondairy fermentation starter for coconut milk or almond milk kefir: add 1/4 cup (60 milliliters) for each can of coconut milk or 2 cups (480 milliliters) almond milk. It's also a nondairy alternative starter to whey that you can use with many of the ferments in this book. Add some fruit and/or flavorings, bottle it, and it will sparkle like soda.

Just under 4 cups (1 liter) filtered water

1/4 cup (60 grams) organic sugar such as evaporated cane crystals or Sucanat

2 tablespoons Water Kefir grains (see Resources, page 183)

Extras: 1/2 to 1 cup (100 to 200 grams) finely chopped fruit, or 1/2 to 1 cup (120 to 240 milliliters) fruit juice, or lemon juice for sparkling lemonade

Bring 2 cups (480 milliliters) of the water to a boil. Remove the pan from the heat and add the sugar; stir to dissolve. Pour into a 1-quart (1-liter) glass jar and add water to fill the jar, leaving 1 inch (2.5 centimeters) of space remaining at the top. Cool completely, then add the kefir grains, cover the jar with a clean dish towel or cloth napkin, and secure it with a rubber band. Leave at room temperature away from sunlight for 24 to 48 hours depending on how sweet you'd like your Water Kefir. At 48 hours most or all of the sugar will be eaten. Your Water Kefir may or may not bubble; either

way is fine—the way to tell if your kefir is working is to taste it. If it tastes less sweet than when you started, it's working. Note that if you are using dried Water Kefir grains it can take a few rounds of kefir making until your grains are fully activated.

Strain into a new container and start another batch of Water Kefir. (If you're not yet ready to make more, make another batch of sugar water, add the kefir grains, and store in the refrigerator. It will keep that way for 2 weeks; if you'd like to keep your kefir on hold longer, feed it a new batch of sugar water and repeat every 2 weeks.) To change things up, you can make every other batch of Water Kefir in coconut water (you'll have to go back to the sugar water after each batch); just add the grains directly to the coconut water and culture it for 24 to 48 hours.

To make Water Kefir soda, pour the Water Kefir into Grolsch-style flip-cap bottles or recycled plastic bottles and add fruit juice in a ratio of 4 parts Water Kefir to 1 part fruit juice. Place in a high-sided storage container, cover with a dish towel, and leave for 2 to 4 days at room temperature. Be very careful when you check your soda: Open it above the sink and always facing away from you as you would do for champagne. Consider using a plastic bottle as a tester; when it feels solid or bulges, it's soda.

Kefir and Kombucha: A Delicious and Diverse Duo

Try a glass filled with half kombucha (page 44) and half dairy kefir (page 39). There's a magical synergy when these two probiotic powerhouses are mixed: The kombucha lightens the kefir and adds a spark of extra effervescence, and the two combine for an increased diversity of beneficial bacteria, resulting in a light yet satisfying everyday drink. Thanks to Gwendalyn Brown for this idea.

FROM TOP: Kombucha (page 44), Water Kefir, and Coconut Water Kefir.

KOMBUCHA:
THE FIZZY PROBIOTIC BEVERAGE OF CHOICE

Makes 1 gallon (4 liters)

In the past decade, kombucha, a fermented tea beverage, has gone from hippie-alternative fringe to big probiotic business. You'll find fans of this sparkling drink at kombucha filling stations in local food co-ops (mine has two brands and six or seven flavors to choose from), while hipsters are discovering kombucha ale on tap in trendy urban bars. But the roots of this fizzy, slightly sweet and tart fermented drink are ancient, dating back to somewhere around the third century B.C., with its first recorded use in China, where it was referred to as an "immortal health elixir." Claims to its health benefits are numerous; top among those benefits are detoxifying the body.

The kombucha culture looks like a slimy pancake. Some call it a mushroom, a fungus, or a "mother"; the technical term is "symbiotic culture of bacteria and yeast," or SCOBY. This yeast-bacteria pancake feeds on a brew of sweetened black or green tea; the bacteria and yeast eat some of the sugar, leaving little left in the finished kombucha. Kombucha feeds on plain old table sugar, so no need to use costly alternative sweeteners for this ferment. Kombucha also needs its caffeine fix, so don't try feeding your SCOBY herbal teas (you can use them to flavor your kombucha later if you like).

There are several good-quality store-bought kombucha brands to choose from, and they are a great convenience and alternative to grabbing a soda on the go, but making your own will save you a lot of money, and once you get the hang of it you'll easily create your own favorite flavors that surpass the limited store selections. Aside from straight-up drinking it, kombucha can be used in countless savory and sweet recipes. Check out Kombucha Brooklyn founders Eric and Jessica Childs's *Kombucha!* for other creative ways to add kombucha to your recipes.

Kombucha, like kefir (page 39), is a living gift, as with every batch of kombucha the "mother" produces a new "baby" culture that calls out to be shared. Look for a kombucha buddy and ask her to pass on one

of her babies (a good place to try is a local chapter of the Weston A. Price Foundation, an organization dedicated to restoring traditional foods to our diets; do an online search to see if there's a group in your area) and then do the same once you've made a few batches. If you're starting from scratch, online sources abound. You'll also need some finished plain kombucha beverage, or "starter tea," for your first batch to jump-start the fermentation process; get some from that same buddy or buy a bottle from a natural foods store or supermarket.

Make sure all equipment and bottles are super clean when you start out to create a welcome environment for the good bacteria while keeping out bad bacteria. Keep an extra SCOBY on hand; if mold forms on your kombucha, toss the batch and SCOBY and start again with your spare.

TOOLS FOR KOMBUCHA MAKING:

- One 1-gallon (4-liter) heatproof glass jar
- Dish towel

INGREDIENTS:

6 caffeinated black or green tea bags

3 1/2 quarts (3.5 liters) filtered water

1 cup (240 grams) white cane sugar

1 kombucha SCOBY (see Resources, page 183)

1 cup (240 milliliters) finished plain kombucha, homemade or store-bought

Put the tea bags in the jar. Bring half of the water to a boil and pour it over the tea bags. Steep for about 10 minutes, then add the sugar and stir until it dissolves. Add the remaining water and cool completely. Remove the tea bags, squeeze the liquid out of them, and add the SCOBY and finished kombucha. Cover the jar with a clean dish towel and secure it with a rubber band.

Set the kombucha in a warm spot for 1 week. Taste it and see if it's ready: It should be bubbly and just a little sweet. If it's too sweet, return it to the warm spot so the culture can continue to eat the sugars, and try it again in a few days. If you let it ferment too long, it will taste like vinegar and you might consider using it in a marinade or dressing instead of drinking it straight.

Remove the "mother" culture along with the "baby" culture it produced (it will be smaller and most likely will be attached to the mother). You may also see cloudy, stringy bits floating in the jar; this is a normal part of fermentation. Make another batch of kombucha or store the cultures submerged in kombucha liquid. Change the liquid every month or so; stored this way the cultures will keep indefinitely.

Recipes starring kombucha:

Wake-up Ketchup (page 74)

Basil-Lime Kombucha Dressing (page 89)

Lemongrass Beef (page 160)

Kombucha Granita (page 177)

Sparkling Berry Salad (page 180)

Bottling Your Kombucha

Your finished kombucha will be lightly effervescent; if you'd like to further carbonate your kombucha, here's how:

Bottle your kombucha straight up, or mix it with fruit juice of your choice or flavoring extracts. Simple vanilla or almond extract is a good option; I'm also a fan of using Medicine Flower super-concentrated flavoring extracts (see Resources, page 183), which come in a unique variety of flavors including green apple, Morello cherry, dark chocolate, and fig. Only a few drops are required.

Another option is to first transfer the kombucha to a clean jar, add herbs, spices, or chopped fruit of your choice, cover with a clean dish towel, and return it to your fermentation area for 1 to 2 days. Strain, then carbonate.

Pour your soon-to-be-carbonated kombucha into glass or recycled plastic bottles or jars with tight-fitting lids (Grolsch-style flip-cap bottles are a good choice), leaving at least 1 inch (2.5 centimeters) clear in each bottle. Place in a high-sided container, cover with a clean dish towel, and set aside in a cool place away from sunlight for 1 to 3 days, depending on the season and kitchen temperature, to build up carbonation.

NOTE: If you opt for glass bottles, take care when opening; always open them over the sink and facing away from you, as if opening a bottle of champagne. For extra precaution, fill a plastic bottle with kombucha as a tester; when the plastic feels completely solid with no give or even starts to bulge, it's ready.

CHAPTER ONE

BREAKFAST

SWEET OR SAVORY MILLET PORRIDGE

FEATURED FERMENT: **FERMENTED MILLET**

Serves 4

Millet becomes surprisingly thick and creamy when it's fermented and then cooked, making it a satisfying breakfast option for folks who are dairy free and those just looking to add more whole grains into their diets. Fermenting millet and other grains lends them a slightly tangy taste, opening up a new world of flavor to your grain-eating experience.

This porridge also becomes the basis for the millet polenta recipe on page 136; to make this a one-pot, two-meal recipe, spoon half into bowls for breakfast, then pour the rest onto a baking sheet to set, keep in the refrigerator, and in the evening make into millet polenta cakes. If this sounds like a plan, you'll need to remember to pour the polenta-cake-bound porridge into the baking sheet as soon as it's cooked, as it starts to set almost immediately.

1 cup (200 grams) millet

2 tablespoons raw apple cider vinegar or other starter culture (see page 20)

1/2 to 3/4 teaspoon fine sea salt

SWEET TOPPING OPTIONS:

Unpasteurized honey or maple syrup

Fresh fruit

Sparkling Berry Salad (page 180)

Tipsy Fruit (page 60)

Coconut Kefir Cream (page 165), Countertop Crème Fraîche (page 79), or yogurt, homemade (page 34) or store-bought

SAVORY TOPPING OPTIONS:

Cultured butter (page 53) and a sprinkling of flaky sea salt

Grated cheddar cheese, scallions, and Live and Kickin' Hot Sauce (page 81)

Fried egg and Salsa Alive (page 76)

Small spoonfuls of miso and a drizzle of toasted sesame oil

Avocado slices and a ripped nori seaweed sheet

Extra-virgin olive oil, diced cucumber, and fresh herbs

Sweet Lemon and Miso Tahini Dressing (page 92)

Rinse the millet in a glass measuring cup until the water runs clear, then drain. Put the millet in a bowl and add the vinegar and 3 cups (720 milliliters) water. Cover with a clean dish towel and set aside for 1 to 2 days to ferment depending on the season and kitchen temperature. It will be ready when it smells just slightly fermented; it won't change all that much. Drain, then transfer the millet to a blender, add 1/2 cup (120 milliliters) water, and blend until the mixture is smooth and thick, adding a little more water if needed. Return the millet to the bowl, cover loosely with a clean dish towel, and set aside to ferment for another 1 to 2 days, until the millet has an aroma somewhere in the vicinity of sourdough.

Pour the fermented millet into a saucepan and whisk in 3 cups (720 milliliters) water. Add 1/2 teaspoon salt if you're making sweet polenta or 3/4 teaspoon salt for savory polenta. Place over medium heat and bring to a simmer; reduce the heat and simmer, whisking frequently, then switching to a wooden spoon as it thickens, for about 10 minutes. Stir almost continuously for the last 2 minutes or so, until very thick and slightly glossy, adding more water to the pan if needed. If it gets too thick and starts to develop lumps, you can whiz it with an immersion blender for a few seconds.

Spoon into bowls and serve with your choice of sweet or savory toppings.

Soaking Grains: A Traditional Fermentation Technique

The grain-based recipes in this book call for fermentation, not specifically to boost good bacteria but to make the grains more digestible and nutritious. Our ancestors fermented their grains (and beans as well) just as they fermented their cabbage for kraut and cucumbers for pickles; just a couple of generations ago the label on the Quaker Oats container called for overnight soaking. Fermenting grains in its simplest form involves soaking them in water, ideally with a starter such as raw apple cider vinegar (see the list of starters on page 19) and then discarding the soaking water, no special equipment or time investment required.

The past couple of decades have seen something of a whole grain fervor, with nutritionists reminding us to include ample grain servings in our daily meals. This well-intentioned advice left out a small but crucial step: soaking or fermenting the grains before cooking them. This is no minor omission, as grains contain a substance called phytic acid in their outer layer or bran, and untreated it can bind with the minerals calcium, magnesium, copper, iron, and zinc and block their absorption in the body. Grains also contain enzyme inhibitors, which can impede digestion. Forward-thinking nutritionists and traditional foods advocates such as Sally Fallon believe that a diet high in unfermented whole grains puts a strain on the digestive system and can result in food allergies and digestive illnesses such as irritable bowel syndrome and Crohn's disease. It has been suggested that the rise in gluten intolerance and now a growing wave of grain intolerance can in part be traced back to this break from how our ancestors prepared their grains.

A simple soak of our grains works to neutralize phytic acid, encourages the production of beneficial enzymes, breaks down enzyme inhibitors and proteins for easier assimilation, and increases vitamin content, particularly vitamin B, encouraging the grains to live up to their superfood potential. Says Sally Fallon in *Nourishing Traditions*, "for a new generation of hardy children, we must return to the breakfast cereals of our ancestors— soaked gruels and porridges." Fermenting your grains takes a little advance planning, but only requires a few minutes to set up, and in the end it will decrease your cooking time. (Soak those oats and there's no need for instant oatmeal packages.) And if you forgot to put the grains up the night before, do it in the morning; even a few hours of soaking will give your grains a world of benefits.

CRUNCHY BUCKWHEAT CEREAL

FEATURED FERMENT: **FERMENTED BUCKWHEAT GROATS**

———————

Makes 2 cups (300 grams)

I quit the cold breakfast cereal habit years ago after learning about extrusion, a method by which grains are subjected to high temperatures and pressure to form them into flakes, puffs, and other cereal shapes. This process causes nutrients to be destroyed and oils to turn rancid, with the resulting cereal offering little sustenance for the day ahead.

This cereal, in which whole buckwheat is fermented for a day or two and then dried until crisp, offers a healthy solution to those wishing to upgrade their breakfast options without going cold turkey on cold cereal. (To me it's reminiscent of my childhood favorite cereal, Grape-Nuts.) You can either dry your buckwheat in a dehydrator to keep the grain's living enzymes and beneficial bacteria alive or toast it in a low oven; either way you'll be getting the digestive benefits of fermentation (see page 49 on why).

Note that despite its name, buckwheat is wheat free; it's actually a fruit seed, related to rhubarb and sorrel. It has a nutty, rich flavor, is a complete vegetarian protein, and even before fermentation may work to boost good bacteria in the gut, making it a welcome addition to any meal and your cultured food lineup.

2 cups (280 grams) untoasted whole buckwheat groats (not kasha, which is toasted and a shade darker)

2 tablespoons raw apple cider vinegar or other starter culture (see page 20)

Rinse the buckwheat in a glass measuring cup until the water runs clear, then drain. Put the buckwheat in a large bowl and add the vinegar and enough filtered water to cover by 2 inches (5 centimeters). Cover with a clean dish towel and set aside to ferment for 1 to 2 days depending on the season and kitchen temperature. It will be ready when it smells just slightly fermented; it won't change all that much. Drain the buckwheat and rinse it very well; you'll notice that the buckwheat has become quite slimy, so make sure to give it a thorough washing (it's okay if you don't get it completely slime free).

If you're making your cereal in a dehydrator, spread the buckwheat in an even layer over two lined dehydrator sheets, set the machine to 145°F (60°C), and dehydrate for 1 hour, then reduce the temperature to 115°F (45°C) and dehydrate for another 3 hours, or until completely dry.

If you're making your cereal in the oven, preheat it to 200°F (95°C). Spread the buckwheat in an even layer over an unlined baking sheet and bake, stirring occasionally, until completely dry but not browned, about 2 hours. Cool and store the cereal in a covered container, and serve as you'd serve any cold breakfast cereal, over yogurt, with milk poured on top, and with fruit slices, maple syrup, and so on.

The cereal will keep for about 3 months, so feel free to scale up the recipe to fill as many sheets as will fit in your dehydrator or oven.

VARIATION

CINNAMON AND BROWN SUGAR BUCKWHEAT CEREAL: Add 6 tablespoons (70 grams) unrefined dark brown sugar and 1/2 teaspoon ground cinnamon to the drained buckwheat before dehydrating or baking.

DEVIL'S FRIED EGGS
WITH BACON AND KIMCHI

FEATURED FERMENTS: **LIVE AND KICKIN' HOT SAUCE, KIMCHI**

———

Serves 2

Here's a trick for cooking bacon that's both crisp and tender: Add some water to the pan as you fry the bacon; as the bacon cooks, the water renders the fat and the bacon comes out evenly crisp yet still tender. This technique also helps avoid the problem of fat splattering from the pan. After you've cooked your bacon you'll take that delicious fat in the pan and fry your eggs in it, then douse the eggs in hot sauce until they are devilishly hot. A side of kimchi completes the experience for a wake-up-your-taste-buds morning meal.

4 strips farmhouse bacon

4 large farm-fresh eggs

Live and Kickin' Hot Sauce (page 81)

Kimchi, homemade (page 25) or store-bought

Put the bacon in a large skillet, preferably cast-iron, and add enough water to completely cover the bottom of the pan. Place over medium-high heat and cook until the water has evaporated, about 8 minutes. Reduce the heat to medium-low and cook until the bacon is crisp, another 5 minutes or so, flipping the slices a couple of times. Divide the bacon between two plates.

Increase the heat to medium-high. Crack the eggs into the skillet and cook until the whites are set, the edges just start to curl up and get a little crisp, and the yolks are perfectly runny or however firm you like them. If the yolks look like they're just about ready but the whites haven't fully cooked, cover the pan for a minute or two to even out the cooking. Place 2 eggs on each plate, add hot sauce to taste, and finish with a generous spoonful of kimchi.

A Note on Bacon Fat

Some liken frying eggs in bacon fat to the work of the devil; I personally favor traditional fats such as lard, butter, and coconut oil that many healthy populations have been raised on (no coincidence, I believe, that fermented foods have played a healthful role in some of those same populations) over processed and rancid vegetable oils. Yes, *rancid* is the word for today's popular shelf-stable vegetable oils: Refined oils including canola oil are in fact rancid when we buy them. They seemingly can last forever, but they've actually expired before they hit the bottle. The reason why is that their flavor components are refined away through high-temperature processes (as is their essential fatty acid content), so we can't detect their rancidity.

SCRAMBLED EGGS
WITH SHORTCUT SALT-CURED SALMON

FEATURED FERMENTS: **SHORTCUT SALT-CURED SALMON,
COUNTERTOP CRÈME FRAÎCHE**

Serves 2

Put up your salmon for curing the night before and you've got the makings of an easy gourmet breakfast. Or even easier, buy prepared gravlax from the fish counter; make sure the package indicates that it is cold smoked rather than hot smoked to ensure that the salmon is only cured and not cooked. The brand Spence & Co. is a good choice.

4 large farm-fresh eggs

Fine sea salt and freshly ground white or black pepper

1 tablespoon cultured butter (see sidebar)

4 slices Shortcut Salt-Cured Salmon (page 129), cut into small pieces

Countertop Crème Fraîche (page 79)

1 tablespoon chopped fresh dill

In a large bowl, vigorously beat the eggs with 2 teaspoons water until light and foamy, then season with salt and pepper and beat lightly.

Melt the butter in a large skillet over medium heat. When the butter starts to bubble, add the eggs. Leave them for about 1 minute, until they begin to set, then using a rubber spatula, gently fold the eggs to form billowy curds; continue to fold until there is no more liquidy egg in the pan but the eggs still look fairly wet, another minute or so. Turn off the heat and fold the eggs a few more times, then divide the eggs between the plates. Top with the salmon, add a dollop of crème fraîche to each serving, and sprinkle the dill on top. Serve immediately.

Cultured Butter

Cultured butter is butter made from cultured cream; bacteria is added to the cream, causing the milk sugars to be converted to lactic acid to infuse the resulting butter with probiotics. Cultured butter has a more developed, fuller flavor—more intensely buttery—than its uncultured cousin. Another example of the magic of fermentation: taking an already delicious food and making it more delicious!

TURKISH-STYLE POACHED EGGS
WITH GARLICKY YOGURT AND SMOKY BUTTER

FEATURED FERMENT: **GREEK YOGURT**
SUPPORTING FERMENTS: **APPLE CIDER VINEGAR, CULTURED BUTTER**

———————

Serves 2

Did you know that the word *yogurt* is neither Greek nor Russian in origin but in fact Turkish? Turkish cuisine is big on strained yogurt, aka Greek yogurt, and this style of serving eggs with yogurt goes back to the time of the Ottomans. For us it's something a little different yet easy to put together for breakfast, with the silkiness of the poached eggs playing against the sourness of the yogurt and the garlic and smoked paprika giving your taste buds something stimulating to savor early in the day. A simple handful of fresh arugula would round out the dish, or for heartier fare you might serve it with a side of millet porridge (page 48) and/or a couple slices of crisp farmhouse bacon.

1 cup (240 milliliters) Greek yogurt, homemade (page 37) or store-bought, at room temperature

2 garlic cloves, pressed through a garlic press

¼ teaspoon fine sea salt, plus more for sprinkling

Large pinch of freshly ground white or black pepper

4 large farm-fresh eggs

2 tablespoons raw apple cider vinegar

2 tablespoons cultured butter (see page 53)

¼ to ½ teaspoon smoked paprika

Pinch of cayenne (optional)

2 tablespoons chopped fresh mint (optional)

2 teaspoons finely chopped pistachios (optional)

Put the yogurt in a small bowl and whisk in the garlic, salt, and pepper. Divide the yogurt mixture between two shallow bowls or rimmed plates.

Break an egg into each of four teacups or small bowls and line a plate with a paper towel. Fill a wide shallow saucepan about two-thirds full with water. Bring to a boil over high heat and add the vinegar.

Lower the heat to very low so the water is just barely simmering. Using the straight end of a wooden spoon, stir to create a whirlpool in the water and gently add 2 of the eggs by lowering the bowls one at a time directly into the water into the center of the whirlpool and gently tipping in the eggs. Cook for about 3 minutes for a soft yolk, about 5 minutes for a hard yolk, creating another whirlpool around the eggs if the whites start to spread out (you'll know the eggs are ready when the white is set and the yolk starts to thicken). Lift the poached eggs out of the water using a slotted spoon and place on the paper towel–lined plate to drain. Repeat with the remaining 2 eggs.

In a small skillet over medium heat, quickly melt the butter with the smoked paprika and cayenne, if using. Let it sizzle for about 1 minute, until the butter just starts to brown.

Place 2 eggs atop the yogurt in each bowl and pour the spiced butter on top of the eggs. Top with a generous pinch of salt and the mint and pistachios, if using, and serve.

BUCKWHEAT PANCAKES

FEATURED FERMENTS: **FERMENTED BUCKWHEAT GROATS, KEFIR**

Serves 4

This is a hearty yet light pancake, with kefir-fermented buckwheat lending a slight sourdough flavor and a sustenance that will keep you satisfied through to lunch. (Turn to page 49 to read why it's important to culture your grains before eating them.) To add berries to your pancakes, gently place a few into each pancake just after pouring the batter into the pan.

1 cup (140 grams) untoasted whole buckwheat groats (not kasha, which is toasted and a shade darker)

2 tablespoons raw apple cider vinegar or other starter culture (see page 20)

1/2 cup (120 milliliters) kefir (dairy, coconut milk, or almond milk; pages 39 to 41) or thinned yogurt, plus more if needed

2 large farm-fresh eggs

1 teaspoon pure vanilla extract

1/4 teaspoon fine sea salt

3/4 teaspoon baking soda

Cultured butter (see page 53) or unrefined virgin coconut oil

TOPPING OPTIONS:

Pats of cultured butter (see page 53)

Maple syrup, unpasteurized honey, or jam

Fresh fruit

Sparkling Berry Salad (page 180)

Tipsy Fruit (page 60)

Coconut Kefir Cream (page 165), Countertop Crème Fraîche (page 79), or yogurt, homemade (page 34) or store-bought

Put the buckwheat in a large bowl. Add the vinegar and 3 cups (710 milliliters) water. Cover with a clean dish towel and leave to ferment for 12 to 24 hours, depending on the season and kitchen temperature. It will be ready when it smells just slightly fermented; it won't change all that much. Drain and rinse well. The buckwheat will be very slimy; try to rinse most of the slime off, but it's okay if you don't get it all. Transfer the buckwheat to a blender, add the kefir, and blend until smooth, adding a little more kefir or water if needed to get it well blended. Transfer to a clean bowl, cover, and set aside to ferment again for another 12 to 24 hours.

Heat a large well-seasoned cast-iron or nonstick skillet over medium heat until hot, 3 to 5 minutes. Meanwhile, mix your batter: Whisk the eggs, vanilla, and salt into the fermented buckwheat. If your batter is too thick, add a little water or kefir. Sprinkle the baking soda over the batter and whisk it in.

Add a generous amount of butter to the pan and brush to coat the skillet evenly. Pour about 1/4 cup (60 milliliters) batter into the skillet for each pancake, making batches of two or three at a time. Cook the pancakes until large bubbles begin to appear and the underside is golden brown, about 2 minutes. Using a thin, wide spatula, flip the pancakes and cook until golden brown on the second side, about 1 1/2 minutes longer. Repeat with the remaining batter, adding more butter to the pan if needed. To keep your pancakes warm until serving time, put the pancakes on a baking sheet in a preheated 200°F (95°C) oven as they come off the skillet. Serve with your choice of toppings.

CHAI SPICE YOGURT LATTE

FEATURED FERMENT: **YOGURT**

Serves 1

The first recipe my husband taught me to make was South Indian–style chai. It was our first date; I invited him over for a farmers' market lunch and he brought with him the fixings for what would become our wake-up and afternoon-break drink for years to come: black tea, ginger, and cardamom. I learned that in his region chai is a two-spice drink (and sometimes no spices at all), none of the cinnamon, black pepper, or cloves found in chai in other parts of India. I liked his simple, everyday version of the beverage, and here it's the basis of an easy-to-make, fully caffeinated, cooling probiotic drink. The serving size is modest, like the roadside sip found everywhere in India, a little something to get you going rather than the oversize meal-in-a-glass chai we often see in coffee shops here.

1 tablespoon loose Assam or other black tea leaves

1 cup (240 milliliters) yogurt, homemade (page 34) or store-bought

3 tablespoons jaggery (see Note, page 69) or maple syrup

2 teaspoons fresh ginger juice (see sidebar)

¼ teaspoon ground cardamom

Put the tea in a mug. Bring ¼ cup (60 milliliters) water to a boil and pour it over the tea. Steep for 3 minutes, then strain through a tea strainer, pressing on the tea leaves to extract all the brewed tea. Cool completely.

In a blender, combine the brewed tea, yogurt, jaggery, ginger juice, and cardamom and blend until well combined. Serve immediately, over ice if you like.

How to Juice Ginger

The easiest way to juice ginger in small amounts is to finely grate it (no need to peel it first) and squeeze it between your fingers to extract the juice; you can wrap the ginger in cheesecloth to make straining easier. A dedicated ceramic grater, a tool with sharp teeth that you run the ginger over to extract the juice while leaving the fiber behind, is another option.

SWAP: Use young coconut yogurt (page 37) for a dairy-free latte.

CHAPTER TWO

BEVERAGES

SPARKLING FRUIT KVASS

Makes about 3 cups (710 milliliters) Sparkling Fruit Kvass
and ¹/2 cup (100 grams) Tipsy Fruit

This effervescent beverage is a healthy, probiotic-rich alternative to canned fruit spritzers and sugary sodas. It's perfect for both seasoned fermenters and those new to the craft, as it requires no starter and takes just minutes to set up. And with every batch you are left with some very juicy fruit, tipsy from soaking in the bubbly juices that form during fermentation; with a little added sweetener you have a no-cooking-needed fruit compote as a bonus, perfect for spooning into cereal or serving as a topping for pancakes (page 56).

Fruit to fill a 1-quart (1-liter) jar by one quarter (see Note)

1 tablespoon unpasteurized honey (see Note)

Flavorings of choice (optional; see combination list below for suggestions)

Filtered water (see Note, page 61)

Put the fruit, honey, and flavorings, if using, in a 1-quart (1-liter) jar. Add filtered water to fill the jar, leaving 1 inch (2.5 centimeters) of space remaining at the top. Tightly cover the jar with a lid or airlock (see page 19) and give it a good shake. Place on a rimmed plate or bowl to catch any potential leakage or bubbling over when you open the lid, cover with a dish towel or cloth napkin, and set aside in a cool place away from sunlight for 2 to 3 days, shaking it once or twice a day. If you see the lid start to bulge at any point, bring it over to the sink and open it with the lid facing away from you, then cover again.

Your kvass is ready when it's bubbling; open it over the sink again and taste it to see if it has fermented to your liking. Note that fruit ferments quickly, so it pays to check on it often, as it can go from lightly fermented to overfermented in a matter of hours (signs of possible overfermentation are a strong alcohol smell and taste, very active bubbling, and a mealy appearance). Strain and serve, or cover and refrigerate to put a chill on it. It will keep for about 2 weeks in the refrigerator.

NOTES: Put delicate berries such as raspberries and blackberries in whole, lightly mash blueberries and citrus, hull and slice strawberries, core and thinly slice apples and pears, and cut dried fruit, grapes, and cherries in half.

Using raw, unpasteurized honey helps to jump-start fermentation.

Sparkling Fruit Kvass combinations:

Blueberries and cinnamon

Peaches and vanilla bean

Nectarines and almond extract

Strawberries and orange zest

TIPSY FRUIT
Makes about ¹/2 cup (100 grams)

Leftover fruit from making Sparkling Fruit Kvass

Maple syrup, unpasteurized honey, or unrefined brown sugar (needed to bring sweetness back to your fruit)

In a bowl, combine the fruit and maple syrup to taste. Serve as you would stewed fruit or compote, perhaps topped with Countertop Crème Fraîche (page 79) or Coconut Kefir Cream (page 165).

BEET KVASS

Makes 1½ quarts (1.5 liters)

This crimson-pink beauty is made from culturing beets and is a whole different taste experience from kvass based on fruit, with fruit kvass sparkling and sweet and beet kvass earthy and salty. The drink hails from eastern Europe, and there are multiple variations—including one made from stale bread.

Beet kvass is refreshing on ice served poolside on a hot day, and the salt makes it replenishing after a good workout. It makes a lively cultured aperitif. It also boasts the benefits of purifying the blood and cleansing the liver. Add a little to Polish-Style Cold Beet Soup (page 110), borscht, or another soup or a salad dressing to give it some extra zing.

2 large beets, scrubbed but not peeled (see Note)

¼ cup (60 milliliters) pickle juice, liquid whey, or other starter culture (optional; page 20)

2 teaspoons fine sea salt

1½ quarts (1.5 liters) filtered water (see Note)

Quarter and slice the beets ⅛ inch (3 millimeters) thick. Put them in a 2-quart (2-liter) glass jar, add the starter, if using, salt, and water, stir well, and cover tightly with a lid or airlock (see page 19). Place on a glass pie plate or rimmed plate to catch any potential leakage or bubbling over when you open the lid, cover with a dish towel, and set aside in a cool spot away from sunlight for 5 to 7 days, until tangy to your liking, removing the towel every couple of days and stirring with a nonmetallic spoon. The drink may form a few bubbles on top, but note that it's not a bubbly drink by nature. Cover and refrigerate your kvass.

When you get to the end of the bottle, it's time to eat the beets! Munch on them or add to a salad or other recipe (if you're not using them right away, store them in kvass to cover to keep them moist). The kvass will keep refrigerated for 2 to 3 months.

NOTES: Scrub your beets well, but don't peel them, as the good bacteria in the peels helps with fermentation.

Make sure to use filtered water, as the chlorine in tap water can interfere with fermentation.

VARIATION

GINGER BEET KVASS: Add ¼ cup (60 milliliters) fresh ginger juice (see page 57 for how to juice ginger) to your kvass before fermenting.

PICKLE MARY

FEATURED FERMENTS: **PICKLE JUICE OR KIMCHI JUICE, CUCUMBER PICKLE, LIVE AND KICKIN' HOT SAUCE**

Serves 1

This take on a virgin Bloody Mary includes a delicious balance of fresh and preserved ingredients: Using home-pressed tomato juice and just-grated horseradish root instead of the bottled varieties transforms your Mary, and pickle juice and kicked-up hot sauce bring a lively assortment of flavors into your glass. Use this drink to showcase your ferments by garnishing with a pickle spear, a pickled carrot stick or two, or any other vegetable you've put up for fermentation. If you'd like to spike your Mary, just add an ounce or two of vodka.

3/4 cup (180 milliliters) fresh tomato juice (see Tip)

1 tablespoon fresh lemon juice

1 to 2 tablespoons pickle juice (page 29) or kimchi juice (page 25)

Dash of Worcestershire sauce

Dash of Live and Kickin' Hot Sauce (page 81)

1 to 2 teaspoons finely grated fresh horseradish (best accomplished on a Microplane grater)

Shake or two of celery salt

Celery rib (optional)

Cucumber Pickles (page 28) or pickled carrot (page 31) spear (optional)

Combine the tomato juice, lemon juice, pickle juice, Worcestershire sauce, hot sauce, horseradish, and celery salt in a jar with a lid. Cover and shake vigorously to combine the ingredients. Taste and adjust the seasonings if needed, adding more hot sauce or horseradish if you'd like more of a kick and more lemon juice if you'd like more brightness. Pour into a glass filled with ice and garnish with the celery, if using, and a pickle spear if you've got one.

TIP: If you've recently made Salsa Alive (page 76), the leftover tomato juice is ready and waiting to be used for your Pickle Mary.

SWITCHEL
(FARMERS' CIDER VINEGAR DRINK)

FEATURED FERMENT: **APPLE CIDER VINEGAR**

———

Serves 1 or 2

Take a swig of switchel and you are connecting with American tradition; this apple cider vinegar–based tonic, also known as Haymaker's punch, goes back to *Little House on the Prairie* days, drunk as an energizer and thirst quencher at a time when soda and lemons for lemonade weren't readily available, and when folks were local by necessity, especially in Vermont during haying season (thus the origin of its alternative name).

The apple cider works to stave off leg cramps (and it's an old Vermont folk cure for aches and pains in general), the maple syrup and molasses are a source of minerals and electrolytes, the ginger helps with digestion, and all of switchel's ingredients are mineral rich, making it a welcome alternative to today's costly and often unnatural energy drinks.

2 tablespoons raw apple cider vinegar

1 tablespoon maple syrup, or to taste

½ teaspoon unsulphured molasses

½ teaspoon fresh ginger juice (see page 57)

Combine all the ingredients with 1 cup (240 milliliters) water in a bottle, cover, and shake to blend (or stir the ingredients directly in a glass). Serve immediately, over ice if you like, or refrigerate until you're ready to drink.

SUPERCHARGE: Substitute Coconut Water Kefir (page 41) for the plain water to make a kefir switchel.

VARIATIONS

SWITCHELADE: Add a couple of squeezes of lemon.

MASTER SWITCHEL: Add a little lemon juice and a pinch of cayenne.

SWITCHEL SODA: Substitute seltzer water for the plain water, stirring instead of shaking.

SPICED WINTER SWITCHEL: Gently heat your switchel (don't let it boil, to ensure your culture stays alive), add warming spices such as nutmeg and cloves, and serve in a mug with a cinnamon stick stirrer.

AVOCADO, DATE, AND ORANGE SHAKE

FEATURED FERMENT: **BUTTERMILK**

———

Serves 2 to 4 (makes about 5 cups/1.2 liters)

Avocado and date are two classic Moroccan ingredients, often blended with milk and served as a creamy, sweet smoothie-type drink. The avocado adds healthy fats and slows down the absorption of the sugar from the fruit, giving greater satiation than the typical all-sweet-fruit smoothie. Buttermilk gives the drink a welcome dose of culture; dairy kefir (page 39) or thinned dairy yogurt (page 34) would also work nicely.

3 cups (710 milliliters) buttermilk, homemade (see page 36) or store-bought

1 cup (240 milliliters) fresh orange juice

4 to 8 dates, to desired sweetness, cut in half, pitted, and soaked in the orange juice for 30 minutes or so

1 small ripe avocado, halved, pitted, and flesh scooped out

Splash of orange flower water (optional)

In a blender, combine all the ingredients and blend until smooth, with no bits of avocado or date visible, adding a little more buttermilk or water if it gets too thick. Serve immediately, over ice if you like.

SWAP: Substitute tangy Almond Milk Kefir (page 41) for the buttermilk for a dairy-free shake.

SUPERCHARGE: Substitute Sparkling Fruit Kvass (page 60) made with oranges for the orange juice.

CHERRY BOUNCE LIQUEUR

Makes about 5 cups (1.2 liters)

When it's cherry season, make it cherry bounce season! This simple recipe, courtesy of *The New Whole Foods Encyclopedia* author Rebecca Wood, transforms the essence of cherries into a tasty liqueur, with the resulting liqueur and cherries as "pickled" as the fruits in kvass (page 60). This ferment is used as a kitchen remedy to counter carpal tunnel syndrome, arthritis, and gout. The history of cherry bounce goes back to George Washington's days: It has been recorded that in September 1784 Washington packed a canteen of cherry bounce for a trip west across the Allegheny Mountains, and Martha Washington was known to serve cherry bounce to company at the president's house.

Rebecca's advice: While you may bounce either sweet or sour cherries, favor sour cherries, as they contain more anti-inflammatory, antioxidant, and pain-relieving properties than sweet cherries. Sour cherries are so meltingly tender and perishable that they bruise at a touch and are thus difficult to find fresh, but not to worry—you can use frozen cherries with equal success. Favor organic cherries, as commercial cherries are one of the fruits highest in pesticide residues.

5 cups (800 grams) fresh sour or sweet cherries (you can substitute unsweetened thawed frozen cherries)

2/3 cup (80 grams) or 1 cup (240 grams) unrefined cane sugar

3 tablespoons fresh lemon juice, if using sweet cherries

1/2 teaspoon ground allspice or cloves (optional)

2 cinnamon sticks (optional)

About 5 cups (1.2 liters) brandy, rum, whiskey, or vodka

If you are using fresh cherries, remove and discard the cherry stems and wash and dry the fruit. For more flavor, leave the pits in (or remove them if you'll later use the cherries). Put them into two 1-quart (1-liter) glass jars. Add 1/2 cup (120 grams) sugar to each jar if you are using sour cherries. If you are using sweet cherries, add 1/3 cup (40 grams) sugar to each jar, along with 1 1/2 tablespoons lemon juice per jar. Add the spices, if using—1/4 teaspoon of the allspice and 1 cinnamon stick to each jar. Cover with brandy, leaving at least 1 inch (2.5 centimeters) space remaining at the top.

Cover tightly and shake to dissolve the sugar (some of it will settle to the bottom—that's okay). Set in a cool spot away from sunlight. Over the next 4 days, invert the jars several times a day to dissolve the sugar, then place the jars in a cool cellar or the refrigerator for 6 to 8 weeks.

Strain, bring the bounce to room temperature, and serve in small cordial glasses or wineglasses. It will keep refrigerated for a year or more.

NOTE: While most of the cherry essence is now in the liqueur, you may enjoy the pitted cherries as a fortified, all-natural version of the maraschino.

SWEET OR SALTY LASSI

FEATURED FERMENT: **YOGURT**

Serves 1

Lassi is a traditional yogurt drink originating in the Punjab region of India. While the sweet version is wildly popular in Indian restaurants here in the States, the savory lassi, salted and flavored with herbs and spices, is actually the more traditional one. Here are recipes for both.

MANGO LASSI

When we first moved to Vermont, my husband, Nash Patel, and I ran a South Indian food stall at the Brattleboro Winter Farmers' Market. Our two top sellers were cultured foods: the fermented lentil and rice crepes known as dosas (page 152) and mango lassi. Sweeten your drink to taste, taking into consideration the tanginess of your current batch of yogurt and the sweetness of your mango.

1 cup (240 milliliters) thin yogurt (see Note), homemade (page 34) or store-bought

1 mango, peeled, flesh cut away from the pit and chopped

1 tablespoon jaggery (see Note), maple syrup, or unrefined brown sugar, or to taste

Pinch of ground cardamom

Pinch of saffron threads

Combine the yogurt, mango, jaggery, and cardamom in a blender and blend until smooth. Pour into a glass, over ice if you like; crush the saffron threads between your fingers into the lassi and stir them in.

NOTES: Stir a little water into your yogurt to give it a drinkable consistency.

Jaggery is an Indian unrefined brown sugar; it is available in Indian groceries, often formed into a cylinder-shaped block.

SWAP: Use dairy kefir (page 39) instead of the yogurt for a tangier lassi or ⅓ cup (80 milliliters) Coconut Milk Kefir (page 41) diluted with ⅔ cup (160 milliliters) water for a coconut milk kefir lassi.

SALTED MINT LASSI

If a salty drink is a new concept for you—if you're not already hooked on beet kvass (page 61)—I encourage you to try this lassi, especially on those days when you're reaching for a cooling beverage but would like to avoid added sugar.

1 cup (240 milliliters) thin yogurt (see Note above), homemade (page 34) or store-bought

Large pinch of fine sea salt, or to taste

Large pinch of ground cumin (optional)

½ small green chile, seeded and minced (optional)

Handful of finely chopped fresh mint leaves

Pour the yogurt into a glass, add the salt, cumin, if using, and chile, if using, and stir to incorporate the seasonings. Stir in the mint and serve, with a couple of ice cubes tossed in if you like.

SWAP: Use dairy kefir (page 39) instead of the yogurt for a tangier lassi or Almond Milk Kefir (page 41) for a nondairy alternative.

CHAPTER THREE

CONDIMENTS AND ACCOMPANIMENTS

JUICED-UP MUSTARD

FEATURED FERMENT: **PICKLE JUICE**

Makes about 1 cup (240 milliliters)

Culturing your own condiments is empowering; it puts you in control of what you spread onto your bread or stir into your otherwise homemade recipes instead of opening a jar and subjecting yourself to the decisions of corporate food manufacturers. Mustard is an easy-to-ferment condiment for you to get started with. This grainy-style mustard uses pickle juice to ferment it and comes out screaming hot but mellows in the refrigerator as it ages. To make it spicier, use more brown mustard seeds than yellow; for milder tastes, up the yellow mustard seeds.

¼ cup (45 grams) yellow mustard seeds

¼ cup (45 grams) brown mustard seeds

½ teaspoon ground turmeric

½ cup (120 milliliters) pickle juice (page 29)

1 tablespoon maple syrup or unpasteurized honey

Pulse the yellow and brown mustard seeds in a blender until coarsely ground. Add the turmeric, pickle juice, and maple syrup to the blender and blend until smooth, or with some mustard seed bits remaining if you like your mustard coarse-grained, adding a little water or more pickle juice, if you have it, if the mixture is too thick. Transfer to a jar, cover tightly, and leave in a cool place away from sunlight for 3 to 4 days, depending on the season and kitchen temperature. The aroma and consistency of the mustard won't really change, but know that the good bacteria are doing their job of infusing the mustard with probiotics just the same.

Transfer to the refrigerator and refrigerate for at least 2 days before using; this allows the flavors to settle and the pungent mustard bite to mellow. The longer you keep it, the more it will mellow. It will keep for about 6 months in the refrigerator.

SWAP: If you are out of pickle juice but you have whey left over from straining yogurt (see page 20) or kombucha (page 44) that has gone a little vinegary, you can use either instead, along with some salt for seasoning.

VARIATIONS

GARLIC MUSTARD: Blend in 2 cloves garlic.
HORSERADISH MUSTARD: Blend in 2 tablespoons grated fresh horseradish.
HONEY MUSTARD: Use honey, increasing the amount to ¼ cup (60 milliliters).

SHORTCUT: Culture store-bought mustard (choose one that is all natural with no sugar added) by adding 1 tablespoon pickle juice or other starter to 1 cup (240 milliliters) mustard; ferment as above.

WAKE-UP KETCHUP

FEATURED FERMENTS: **KOMBUCHA, APPLE CIDER VINEGAR**

———

Makes 1 pint (480 milliliters)

To make this all-natural, no-high-fructose-corn-syrup-containing ketchup, we're going to employ a little fermentation resuscitation: We'll open a jar of tomato paste, add a starter, and culture it back to life!

2 (7-ounce/200-gram) jars tomato paste

3 tablespoons unpasteurized honey or maple syrup

¼ cup (60 milliliters) plain kombucha, homemade (page 44) or store-bought

1½ tablespoons raw apple cider vinegar

½ teaspoon fine sea salt

¼ teaspoon ground allspice

Pinch of ground cloves

Spoon out 2 tablespoons of the tomato paste and reserve it to use in another recipe.

In a medium bowl, whisk together all the ingredients until smooth. Spoon the mixture into a glass pint jar, leaving at least 1 inch (2.5 centimeters) space remaining at the top. Cover loosely and leave in a cool place away from sunlight for 3 to 5 days to ferment. Uncover the ketchup, give it a stir, then cover again and store in the refrigerator, where it will keep for several months.

Culturing Your Condiments

To culture store-bought ketchup, pour out about ½ cup (120 milliliters) of the ketchup from the bottle it came in and add 2 tablespoons kombucha, liquid whey, or other starter (page 20); shake to mix it in. Ferment as in the ketchup recipe above. (Choose a brand without high-fructose corn syrup and one that comes in a glass bottle.)

This is a shortcut method of fermentation you can try out with other store-bought condiments, such as salsa, mustard, hot sauce, even peanut butter and jelly, bringing new life to many of the canned, jarred, and packaged products lining your pantry shelves.

A rule of thumb: Always start with unprocessed, additive-free foods, as preservatives and the like can interfere with fermentation; avoid foods with a high vinegar content; and have on hand a starter (a starter isn't optional for foods that have been cooked, as their enzymes have been destroyed) that matches the flavors of your food. Pickle juice (page 29), kimchi juice (page 25), Water Kefir (page 42), liquid whey (page 20), and kombucha (page 44) are common starters.

SALSA VERDE

Makes about 1 quart (1 liter)

Sweet, spicy, slightly sour, and with a distinctly fresh flavor, this salsa gets scooped onto chips and spooned onto scrambled eggs, and tops fish tacos (page 143), pork stew (page 161), and just about any other savory dish. Late summer, when tomatillos come into season, is when I make my salsa verde, scaling up the recipe to keep me stocked well into winter. If you'd like to jump-start fermentation, add ¼ cup (60 milliliters) liquid whey or other starter (page 20) and decrease the amount of salt to 1 tablespoon.

2 pounds (900 grams) tomatillos

1 onion, chopped

1 to 2 jalapeño chiles, seeded if you like, chopped

2 garlic cloves, halved

1½ tablespoons fine sea salt

Leaves and tender stems of ½ bunch fresh cilantro, chopped

Remove and discard the papery husks from the tomatillos, rinse them well, and pat dry. Cut each tomatillo in half. Combine the tomatillos, onion, chiles, garlic, and salt in a food processor or blender and process until smooth or pulse in a food processor for a chunkier salsa. Pulse in the cilantro.

Transfer the sauce to a 1-quart (1-liter) jar, leaving at least 1 inch (2.5 centimeters) of space remaining at the top. (If there is too much for one jar, put the extra in a smaller jar.) Cover tightly with a lid or airlock (see page 19), place the jar on a rimmed plate (a glass pie plate works nicely) to catch any potential leakage or bubbling over when you open the lid, cover with a clean dish towel, and set aside in a cool place away from sunlight to ferment for 3 to 5 days, depending on the season and kitchen temperature, until the salsa is tangy to your liking. As your salsa ferments, open the jar every day, holding it over the sink as you do so to release pent-up gases and catch any potential bubbling over. When the salsa is ready, transfer it to the refrigerator, where it will keep for up to 6 months.

VARIATION

CHIPOTLE SALSA VERDE: Omit the jalapeños and add ½ to 1 teaspoon ground chipotle chile.

SALSA ALIVE

Makes 1 quart (1 liter)

Here's a happy upgrade to your chips and salsa dipping repertoire and a smart switch-up for any recipe that calls for jarred salsa. Mix it into avocado and you're set for guacamole (page 116), or top your tacos (page 143) with some for a lively finish. Salsa Alive is a good preservation alternative to canning or freezing your bumper crop of late-summer tomatoes. If you'd like to jump-start fermentation, add ¼ cup (60 milliliters) liquid whey or other starter (page 20) and decrease the amount of salt to 2 teaspoons.

4 large tomatoes, peeled, seeded, and finely chopped (see Notes)

1 red, yellow, or white onion, finely chopped

1 to 2 jalapeño chiles, seeded if you like, finely chopped

Leaves and tender stems from 1 small bunch fresh cilantro, chopped

2 garlic cloves, minced

Juice of 2 limes, or to taste

1 tablespoon fine sea salt

In a large bowl, combine all the ingredients. Transfer to a 1-quart (1-liter) wide-mouth jar. Press down until the juices rise up; if there is not enough liquid to cover the vegetables, add a little water and make sure there is at least 1 inch (2.5 centimeters) of space remaining at the top. (If there is too much for one jar, put the extra in a smaller jar.) Cover tightly with a lid or airlock (see page 19), place the jar on a rimmed plate (a glass pie plate works nicely) to catch any potential leakage or bubbling over when you open the lid, cover with a clean dish towel, and set aside in a cool place away from sunlight to ferment for about 2 days, depending on the season and kitchen temperature.

The salsa is ready when it is tangy to your liking (tomatoes are fast fermenters and continue to ferment in the refrigerator a bit, so be sure to check on your salsa often; signs of possible overfermentation are a strong alcohol smell and taste, very active bubbling, and a mealy appearance). Transfer to the refrigerator, where it will keep for about 2 months. Note that this salsa may be more liquidy than standard salsa; if so, scoop it from the jar using a slotted spoon.

NOTES: To peel tomatoes: Using a paring knife, cut an X on the bottom of each tomato and slip them into a small pan of boiling water for about 30 seconds. Scoop them out with a slotted spoon and the skin will peel off easily. To scoop the seeds out, hold the cut half of a tomato in your hand and squeeze gently, then use a spoon or your fingers to scoop out the seeds.

Put the seeds in a strainer set atop a bowl and press on the seeds to extract the tomato juice. Drink it as is, or use it as the base for a Pickle Mary (page 63).

SHORTCUT: If you find all-natural fresh salsa in the refrigerated section of the market, there's nothing to stop you from culturing it! Add some salt, whey, or another starter and ferment as described above.

FROM TOP: Salsa Verde (page 75); Salsa Alive (above); and Smoky Peach, Cherry Tomato, and Basil Salsa (page 78).

SMOKY PEACH, CHERRY TOMATO, AND BASIL SALSA

Makes about 1 quart (1 liter)

Fruit is a fast fermenter and continues to ferment in the refrigerator a bit, so be sure to check on your salsa at least once a day (signs of possible overfermentation are a strong alcohol smell and taste, very active bubbling, and a mealy appearance). Peel your peaches in the same way you'd peel tomatoes (see page 76). Mangos could be used in place of the peaches. If you'd like to jump-start fermentation, add ¼ cup (60 milliliters) liquid whey or other starter (page 20) and decrease the amount of salt to 2 teaspoons.

- 1 pound (450 grams) peaches (about 3 large), peeled and chopped
- 1 pint (about 1 pound/450 grams) cherry tomatoes, cut in half, seeds squeezed out
- 1 tablespoon fine sea salt
- Handful of fresh basil leaves, minced
- Juice of 2 lemons

In a large bowl, combine all the ingredients. Transfer to a 1-quart (1-liter) wide-mouth jar. Press down until the juices rise up; if there is not enough liquid to cover the fruit, add a little water and make sure there is at least 1 inch (2.5 centimeters) of space remaining at the top. (If there is too much for one jar, put the extra in a smaller jar.) Cover tightly with a lid or airlock (see page 19), place the jar on a rimmed plate (a glass pie plate works nicely) to catch any potential leakage or bubbling over when you open the lid, cover with a clean dish towel, and set aside in a cool place away from sunlight to ferment for about 2 days, depending on the season and kitchen temperature.

  The salsa is ready when it is tangy to your liking. Transfer to the refrigerator, where it will keep for up to 2 months. This salsa may be more liquidy than standard salsa; if so, scoop it from the jar using a slotted spoon.

SWEET MANGO CHUTNEY

Makes 1 quart (1 liter)

This chutney makes a starring appearance in the collard green wrap on page 135 and can also be spooned over chicken or fish or served alongside pork chops and any number of Indian dishes.

- 4 cups (about 3 pounds/1.4 kilograms) peeled and cubed ripe mangos (4 large)
- ¼ cup (60 milliliters) Water Kefir (page 42) or other starter culture (page 20) or an additional 1½ teaspoons fine sea salt
- ¼ cup (60 milliliters) fresh lime juice
- ¼ cup (60 grams) jaggery (see Note, page 69) or maple syrup
- 2 teaspoons grated fresh ginger
- 1½ teaspoons fine sea salt
- ¼ teaspoon ground cardamom
- ¼ teaspoon ground cinnamon
- ¼ teaspoon ground cayenne
- Pinch of ground cloves
- ¼ cup (35 grams) raisins

Put the mangos in a large bowl and lightly pound them with a kitchen pounder to bring out the juices and reduce the volume by almost half. In a separate bowl, combine the starter, if using, lime juice, jaggery, ginger, salt, cardamom, cinnamon, cayenne, and cloves, stirring to dissolve the jaggery. Stir the mixture into the mangos, add the raisins, then pack into a 1-quart (1-liter) glass jar, leaving at least 1 inch (2.5 centimeters) of space at the top. Cover tightly, place the jar on a rimmed plate to catch any potential leakage or bubbling over when you open the lid, and leave to ferment in a cool place away from sunlight for 2 to 3 days, until bubbly and tangy to your liking, checking on it a couple of times a day and opening it to release any gases and stirring it. Cover and refrigerate until ready to use. If the chutney is liquidy when you go to serve it, scoop it out using a slotted spoon.

COUNTERTOP CRÈME FRAÎCHE

Makes a little more than 2 cups (480 milliliters)

Crème fraîche is heavy cream naturally thickened by friendly bacteria; the cream is mixed with buttermilk or yogurt and left to ferment at room temperature until it's slightly soured and deliciously creamy, with a satisfyingly higher fat content and subtler, more complex flavor than sour cream. It is a ferment of choice in French cooking, where it is used to thicken sauces and soups. The high fat content means you can cook with it without fear of it separating, though to keep its friendly bacteria live, I prefer to add it just at the end of cooking.

Crème fraîche is a wonderful topping for fresh fruit and cake in place of the standard whipped cream and a change of pace from yogurt or sour cream. I use it in ice cream (page 172), atop Shortcut Salt-Cured Salmon (page 129), and spread over bread instead of mayonnaise. Historically the cream is unpasteurized (French laws are much more liberal than U.S. regulations when it comes to raw milk ferments like crème fraîche and cheeses), with the naturally occurring bacteria preventing spoilage and thickening the cream. Here it's your choice whether to use raw or pasteurized milk depending on preference and availability in the state you live in (see Live Yogurt Start to Finish, page 36).

2 cups (480 milliliters) heavy cream

¼ cup (60 milliliters) homemade or store-bought buttermilk (see page 36) or yogurt (page 34) or crème fraîche from your last batch

In a glass jar, bowl, or other nonreactive container, mix together the cream and buttermilk to incorporate. Loosely cover and set aside on the countertop for 12 to 24 hours, depending on the season and kitchen temperature, until a thick, creamy, slightly tangy crème fraîche is born. Stir again, cover, and store in the refrigerator, where it will keep (and continue to thicken a bit) for up to 2 weeks.

VARIATIONS

SIMPLE SWEET CRÈME FRAÎCHE: Add 2 to 3 tablespoons finely ground unrefined granulated sugar or powdered sugar to your finished crème fraîche.

VANILLA CRÈME FRAÎCHE: Add 2 teaspoons pure vanilla extract or the seeds of 1 vanilla bean to your finished crème fraîche. Toss the spent pod into a jar of sugar and leave it there for a week or two to subtly scent a future batch of sweet crème fraîche.

MAPLE CRÈME FRAÎCHE: Add 2 to 3 tablespoons maple syrup to your finished crème fraîche.

WHIPPED CRÈME FRAÎCHE: Whip your crème fraîche, sweetened, flavored, or plain, using an electric mixer until soft peaks form (it will not form stiff peaks).

LIVE AND KICKIN' HOT SAUCE

Makes about 2 cups (480 milliliters)

Caution: This sauce starts kickin' from the moment the chiles start moving in the food processor; to keep it contained, cover the machine with a towel as you process and avoid taking a big inhale of the fiery fumes as you open the container. And the first couple of times you reach for the bottle, open it slowly and refrain from shaking it, as it's super-alive and can bubble over. If dairy is part of your diet, you could use whey instead of the pickle juice for your starter; Beet Kvass (page 61) or Water Kefir (page 42) also make good starters. Experiment with the type of chiles, from jalapeño to habanero, or mix and match chiles to make a signature hot sauce blend.

1½ pounds (680 grams) your choice of chiles, stemmed but retaining green tops, seeded if you like a milder hot sauce

1½ tablespoons unrefined cane sugar (optional)

1 teaspoon fine sea salt

2 tablespoons pickle juice (page 29) or sauerkraut brine (page 23)

In a food processor, combine the chiles, sugar, if using, salt, and pickle juice and process until completely broken down, scraping the sides of the machine once or twice as needed. Transfer to a 1-quart (1-liter) glass jar, leaving at least 1 inch (2.5 centimeters) of space remaining at the top. Cover tightly with a lid or airlock (see page 19), place the jar on a rimmed plate (a glass pie plate works nicely) to catch any potential leakage or bubbling over when you open the lid, cover with a clean dish towel, and set aside in a cool place away from sunlight to ferment for 3 to 7 days, depending on the season and kitchen temperature, until bubbly and fermented to your liking.

As the sauce is fermenting, open the jar every day, holding the jar over the sink as you do so to release pent-up gases. When the hot sauce is ready, strain it through a fine-mesh strainer into a bowl, pressing on the solids with the back of a spoon to extract all the juices. Funnel the sauce into a bottle, cover, and place in the refrigerator, where it will keep for about a year.

NOTE: Save the pulp that remains after straining—it's a chile paste that you can use to flavor sauces and other recipes.

VARIATIONS

LIVE AND KICKIN' GARLIC HOT SAUCE: Add 2 or 3 garlic cloves as you process the chiles.

CULTURED MAYONNAISE

Makes about 1¼ cups (300 milliliters)

If you want good mayonnaise, there's no way around it: You'll have to make it yourself. Culturing your from-scratch mayo rewards your efforts because it extends the condiment's refrigerated shelf life from the standard five days to up to three weeks.

Some people like the strong flavor of olive oil in their mayonnaise; others prefer a neutral-tasting oil for its blank canvas qualities, and for some a mixture of the two is a happy medium. The choice is yours, but stick to unrefined oils for the healthiest mayonnaise. Since we're using raw eggs for this recipe, we leave the mayonnaise out at room temperature for a short fermentation period of just a few hours rather than a few days.

2 large farm-fresh egg yolks, at room temperature (see Note)

1 tablespoon raw apple cider vinegar

1 tablespoon cold (see Note) liquid whey or other starter culture (page 20)

1 teaspoon Juiced-up Mustard (page 73), or ¼ teaspoon yellow mustard powder

¼ teaspoon fine sea salt

1 cup (240 milliliters) unrefined oil, such as extra-virgin olive, safflower, sesame, sunflower, or avocado oil, at room temperature

In a medium bowl, whisk together the egg yolks, vinegar, whey, mustard, and salt, until frothy. Pour the oil into a liquid measuring cup and very slowly, whisking the whole time, add the oil to the egg yolk mixture, first drop by drop for the first ½ cup (120 milliliters)—at this point it should be the consistency of heavy cream. Then pour in the remaining oil in a thin, slow stream. A little patience is needed, but this is the only way your mayonnaise will come together; in the end it'll be just 3 or 4 minutes out of your life.

Alternatively, make your mayonnaise in a food processor or blender, adding the oil very slowly through the feed tube as the machine is running. Transfer the mayonnaise to a pint jar, making sure there is at least 1 inch (2.5 centimeters) space remaining at the top. Cover tightly and leave in a cool dark place to ferment for 7 to 12 hours, the lesser time on a warm day. Refrigerate until ready to use.

NOTE: The mayonnaise won't set if your ingredients are cold—except for the cold whey. Adding cold whey to the yolks before whisking in the oil helps create a stronger emulsion and ensure a successful mayonnaise.

VARIATIONS

PRESERVED LEMON MAYONNAISE: Omit the salt and whisk in 1½ tablespoons minced preserved lemon peel (page 100) at the end.

MISO MAYONNAISE: Omit the salt and whisk in 1 tablespoon light miso at the end.

SALTED PLUM MAYONNAISE: Omit the salt and whisk in 1 tablespoon umeboshi paste at the end.

CREAMY CASHEW CHEESE

Makes about 2 cups (500 grams)

Cheese is fermented by nature, and there are many books devoted to the craft of cheesemaking; Jeff Cox's recent *Essential Book of Fermentation* contains an informative exploration on the subject. While I leave the dairy cheese to the experts, in this chapter I've included three simple recipes for fermented cheeses based on nuts. Any home cook can easily pull off these cheeses without specialized cheesemaking skills or equipment. Unlike dairy cheese, cashew cheese tastes perfect straight from the fridge.

3 cups (400 grams) raw cashews

½ cup (120 milliliters) filtered water

1 teaspoon fine sea salt

2 teaspoons probiotic powder (see Note)

Fresh lemon juice if needed

Rinse the cashews in a glass measuring cup until the water runs clear. Soak the cashews in a bowl with water to cover by a couple of inches for 2 to 4 hours, then drain and rinse.

In a food processor, combine the cashews, filtered water, and salt and blend until very smooth, about 5 minutes, scraping down the sides and resting every couple of minutes to keep from overheating the machine. Briefly process in the probiotic powder just to incorporate it.

Transfer the mixture to a bowl, cover with a dish towel or plate, and leave in a warm place away from sunlight to ferment for 2 to 4 days depending on the season and kitchen temperature, until it has a pleasantly sour smell to it (check it every day to see how it's coming along). To jump-start fermentation, ferment in a food dehydrator set to 90°F (30°C) for 12 to 14 hours. Return the cheese to the food processor and process until silky smooth and a little glossy, and the mixture forms a ball in the machine. Taste, and if the cheese is in need of a little perkiness, pulse in some lemon juice.

Transfer to a container, cover, and store in the refrigerator, where it will keep for up to 1 week.

NOTE: Probiotic powder can be found in the refrigerated area of your natural food store's supplement section; choose a brand labeled *dairy-free* to keep your cheese dairy free. If you have probiotic capsules, you can open a few and use them instead of buying the powder.

SWAP: Substitute ½ teaspoon nondairy yogurt starter culture (see Resources, page 183) for the probiotic powder and ferment the cashew cheese in a yogurt maker for 12 to 14 hours.

VARIATIONS

SCALLION CREAM CHEESE: Stir in 2 minced scallions (light and green parts), 1½ teaspoons onion powder, and 1½ teaspoons garlic powder at the end.

HERBED CREAM CHEESE: Stir in 1 tablespoon minced fresh herbs, such as basil, thyme, oregano, and/or rosemary, at the end. You could also add the herbs to the scallion cream cheese variation above.

FRUITY CREAM CHEESE: Reduce the salt to ½ teaspoon and at the end stir in ¼ cup (50 grams) Tipsy Fruit (page 60) and a little fresh lemon or lime juice if you like. Fresh fruit will work too, as will a fruit jam (in which case, skip the sweetener).

ALL-AROUND ALMOND CHEESE

Makes about 1 1/2 cups (375 grams)

To create this cultured nondairy cheese, you'll first make almond milk; the leftover blended nuts from making the milk become the base for the almond cheese: two recipes out of one. One extra step is required: You'll need to peel the almonds (if you're just making the milk, peeling isn't required); after a good overnight soak, place an almond between your forefinger and thumb, squeeze, and the peel should pop right off (if it doesn't, pour some hot water over the almonds, let them soak for a few minutes more, and try again). Unlike dairy cheese, almond cheese tastes perfect straight from the fridge.

Leftover blended almonds from making 1 recipe Almond Milk (about 3/4 cup/130 grams; page 38)

1 1/2 teaspoons probiotic powder (see Note, page 83)

1/2 cup (120 milliliters) extra-virgin olive oil or other unrefined oil

1 1/2 teaspoons onion powder

1 1/2 teaspoons garlic powder

1/2 teaspoon fine sea salt, or to taste

1/4 teaspoon freshly ground black pepper

Fresh lemon juice, if needed

Make the almond milk as directed; as you strain the almond milk through cheesecloth or a nut milk bag, squeeze the nut pulp well to remove excess milk. Transfer the pulp to a bowl, work the probiotic powder in with a fork or your hands (make sure they are super-clean or wear disposable gloves), cover with a dish towel or plate, and leave in a warm place away from sunlight for 2 to 4 days depending on the season and kitchen temperature, until it has a pleasantly sour smell to it (check it every day to see how it's coming along). To jump-start fermentation, ferment in a food dehydrator set to 90°F (30°C) for 12 to 14 hours.

Transfer the fermented nut pulp to a food processor, add the probiotic powder, oil, onion and garlic powder, salt, and pepper, and process for about 5 minutes, until very creamy, stopping the machine a few times to scrape the sides and to keep the cheese and machine from getting too hot. Taste and season with more salt and/or some lemon juice if needed. Spoon the cheese into a container, cover, and place in the refrigerator, where it will keep for up to 1 week.

SWAP: Substitute 1/2 teaspoon nondairy yogurt starter culture (see Resources, page 183) for the probiotic powder and ferment the almond cheese in a yogurt maker for 12 to 14 hours.

VARIATIONS

SIMPLE ALMOND CHEESE: For a plainer version that pairs well with jam and other sweet spreads, omit the onion powder, garlic powder, and pepper.

ALMOND CHEESE LOGS: Roll the finished cheese into log shapes of any size and press herbs or cracked black pepper into them if you like. If you have a dehydrator, place the logs in the machine, set it to 115°F (45°C), and dehydrate for about 6 hours to form a rind.

MISO PARMESAN

Makes about 1¹/2 cups (225 grams)

I like to have some fun with my ferments, using them in new and unexpected ways, like creating this take on Parmesan based on miso. It's so simple, because you don't have to make the miso yourself! Just find a brand that you like that's labeled "unpasteurized" or "raw" and you're good to go. Here in New England I buy South River Miso, a western Massachusetts–based handcrafted, wood-fired miso company that makes miso the old-fashioned way, in cypress vats with workers stomping on the soybeans to mash them into paste.

This recipe gets its cue from the raw food world, where cashews become cheese through the craft of fermentation and the process of dehydration. You'll need a dehydrator and a good chunk of time for this recipe (and note that drying times can vary widely), but the prep time is only a few minutes, and if you become a fan of this ferment, you could easily double or triple the recipe to keep you flush in Parm for months at a stretch. If you don't have a dehydrator and your oven can be set to a low temperature (under 200°F/95°C), you can experiment with drying it in the oven.

Sprinkle your Parm over pasta, toss some into a salad, spoon over scrambled eggs; use it anywhere you would use dairy Parmesan.

2 cups (210 grams) cashew pieces

1 cup (240 grams) light miso

Rinse the cashews in a glass measuring cup until the water runs clear. Soak the cashews in a bowl with water to cover by a couple of inches (about 5 centimeters) for 4 hours, then drain and rinse well. Put the cashews in a food processor, add the miso, and process until smooth, 2 to 3 minutes.

Using a rubber spatula, spread the mixture very thinly over two lined dehydrator sheets (it will take a bit of time to get evenly spread; you'll need to move the spatula up and down the sheet in both directions a few times to get the job done properly).

Set the machine to 145°F (62°C), and dehydrate for 3 hours. Reduce the temperature to 115°F (45°C) and dehydrate for another 10 hours or so, until the cheese is dry enough that it can be peeled off the sheet. Flip the cheese directly onto a mesh dehydrator screen and dehydrate for another 7 hours or so, until completely dry. Remove from the dehydrator and cool completely.

Crumble the cheese into flakes or process in a food processer to a coarse powder. Store in an airtight container for up to 3 months.

SWAP: Use hulled pumpkin seeds instead of the cashews for a more intensely nutty flavor.

CHAPTER FOUR

SALADS AND DRESSINGS

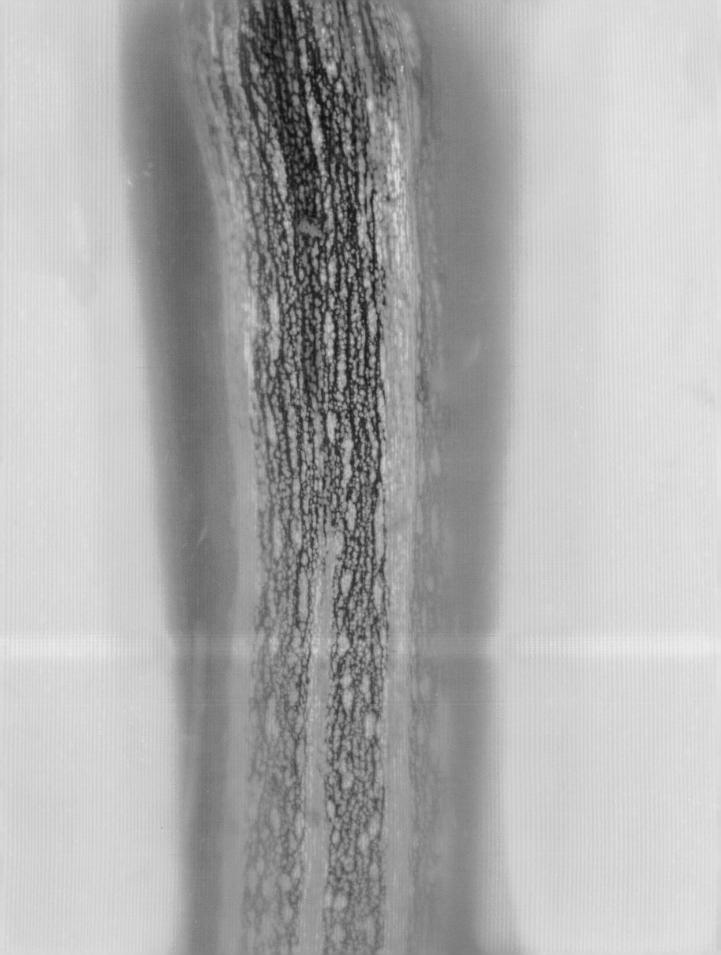

HONEY CIDER VINAIGRETTE

Makes 1 cup (240 milliliters)

This is my house cultured dressing, one that hits all the flavor bases and serves as a reliable accompaniment to any bowl of greens.

1/4 cup (60 milliliters) raw apple cider vinegar

2 tablespoons fresh lemon juice

2 tablespoons unpasteurized honey or maple syrup

2 teaspoons Juiced-up Mustard (page 73)

1 to 2 garlic cloves, pressed through a garlic press

2 teaspoons minced fresh herbs of choice, or
   1 teaspoon dried herbs

3/4 teaspoon fine sea salt

1/4 teaspoon freshly ground black pepper

3/4 cup (180 milliliters) extra-virgin olive oil

Combine all the ingredients in a jar, cover, and shake until the dressing is emulsified.

Alternatively, in a medium bowl, whisk all the ingredients except the oil until well incorporated, then whisk in the oil until emulsified. It will keep in a covered in the refrigerator for 3 to 4 days.

SALTED PLUM VINAIGRETTE

FEATURED FERMENT:
UMEBOSHI VINEGAR

Makes just over 3/4 cup (180 milliliters)

The umeboshi, a Japanese plum that's fermented through salt preservation, boasts a pretty pink color and a tart, salty, fruity flavor. It shows itself as an ingredient in a variety of dressings, sauces, and other dishes: I use it as flavoring for my Mexican corn (page 127), it tops a bowl of congee (page 105), and umeboshi paste can be spread over cooked corn on the cob instead of butter and salt.

Umeboshi vinegar technically isn't a vinegar because it contains salt, but this inherent saltiness means one less step in making your vinaigrette: Just mix it with olive oil and it's practically instant dressing, no seasoning required (the optional ingredients give it a little something extra) and no more reason to rely on convenient yet costly store-bought bottles of dressing. Dress any salad with this vinaigrette or toss with cabbage, cooked kale, or other hearty greens. Umeboshi vinegar can be found in Japanese groceries and natural food stores in the vinegar section.

1/2 cup (120 milliliters) extra-virgin olive oil

2 tablespoons umeboshi vinegar

2 tablespoons mirin (Japanese rice wine; optional)

1 tablespoon rice vinegar (optional)

1 1/2 teaspoons minced fresh herbs of choice, or
   3/4 teaspoon dried herbs (optional)

Freshly ground black pepper to taste

In a small jar with a lid, combine all the ingredients, cover, and shake until emulsified. Shake again just before serving. The vinaigrette will keep in the refrigerator for up to 2 weeks (without herbs).

BASIL-LIME KOMBUCHA
DRESSING

FEATURED FERMENT: **KOMBUCHA**

———

Makes just over 3/4 cup (180 milliliters)

Kombucha, with its tart taste and slightly astringent qualities, has been likened to cider vinegar, and in fact can take the place of vinegar in any number of dressings. This dressing works with fresh-from-the-bottle store-bought kombucha, and it's also a clever way to make use of overly sour kombucha. When you've let a batch of kombucha go a little too long, when it turns from drinking-ready to pucker-your-mouth vinegary, don't toss it: Bottle it, label it KOMBUCHA VINEGAR, and add it to your DIY fermentation repertoire. This dressing is perfect with any green salad.

1/4 cup (60 milliliters) plain kombucha, homemade (page 44) or store-bought

1 tablespoon fresh lime juice, or to taste

1 tablespoon unpasteurized honey (optional)

1 garlic clove, cut into quarters

1/2 teaspoon fine sea salt, or to taste

1/4 teaspoon freshly ground black pepper

1/2 cup (120 milliliters) extra-virgin olive oil

1/2 cup (20 grams) finely chopped fresh basil leaves

In a blender, combine the kombucha, lime juice, honey, garlic, salt, and pepper and blend until the mixture is combined and the garlic is minced. With the machine still running, slowly add the oil through the hole in the lid and blend until emulsified. Add the basil and blend for a few seconds, until well incorporated (don't overblend or the basil will lose its vibrant green color). Taste and add more lime juice and/or salt if needed. It will keep in a covered jar in the refrigerator for 3 to 4 days.

KIMCHI, SCALLION, AND TOASTED SESAME OIL
DRESSING

FEATURED FERMENT: **KIMCHI JUICE**

———

Makes 1/2 cup (120 milliliters)

Kimchi juice, the brine left at the bottom of the kimchi jar, is a valuable flavoring, at once intensely salty, sour, and spicy. This dressing is ideal for marinating cucumbers, or try tossing it with some raw cabbage for a fresh variation on kimchi.

1/4 cup (60 milliliters) kimchi juice (page 25), plus more if needed

1/2 teaspoon toasted sesame oil

1 scallion, white and green parts, minced

1/4 cup (60 milliliters) unrefined plain sesame oil or extra-virgin olive oil

Rice vinegar, if needed

Fish sauce or salt, if needed

Combine the kimchi juice, toasted sesame oil, scallion, and plain sesame oil in a jar, cover, and shake until the dressing is emulsified. Alternatively, in a medium bowl, whisk the kimchi juice, toasted sesame oil, and scallion until well incorporated, then whisk in the plain sesame oil until emulsified. Taste and add more kimchi juice or some rice vinegar and fish sauce or salt if needed, depending on how highly seasoned your current batch of kimchi is. It will keep in a covered jar in the refrigerator for 3 to 4 days.

BIBB LETTUCE SALAD
WITH CREAMY GORGONZOLA DRESSING

FEATURED FERMENTS: **DAIRY KEFIR**
SUPPORTING FERMENT: **APPLE CIDER VINEGAR**

Serves 4

This easy-to-assemble salad makes a pretty presentation, with the Bibb lettuce leaves cleaned then reassembled to look like a whole head of lettuce and drizzled with a creamy dressing. The blue cheese dressing uses kefir instead of the standard mayonnaise or sour cream for a tangy take on a classic; it could also be made with regular or Greek yogurt if that's what you have on hand. For the Gorgonzola, use Gorgonzola dolce rather than Gorgonzola piccante, as the dolce is creamier and aged less and blends well into the dressing.

DRESSING
(MAKES ABOUT 1 CUP/240 MILLILITERS)

¾ cup (180 milliliters) dairy kefir (page 39)

⅓ cup packed soft Gorgonzola cheese (about 1½ ounces/40 grams), at room temperature

1 garlic clove, pressed through a garlic press

2 teaspoons raw apple cider vinegar

2 teaspoons fresh lemon juice

½ teaspoon fine sea salt, or to taste

¼ teaspoon coarsely ground black pepper, or to taste

SALAD

4 small heads Bibb lettuce

1 large tomato, cored, seeded, and diced

2 tablespoons pine nuts, toasted

Make the dressing: In a medium bowl, combine all the ingredients and whisk with a fork until mostly smooth with some small bits of Gorgonzola cheese remaining.

Make the salad: Cut the core from each head of lettuce and separate the leaves, but keep the leaves from each head together. Rinse the leaves by placing them in a bowl of cold water. Lift them out and into a salad spinner and spin them dry. Stack the leaves on plates to form a flower shape (like your original head of lettuce) starting with the largest leaves on the bottom to form a base and finishing with the smaller leaves. Repeat with the remaining lettuce.

Drizzle the dressing (you may have leftover dressing—see Tip) over the lettuce (thin it with a little water if it's not pourable) and scatter the diced tomato and pine nuts between the leaves. Serve immediately.

TIP: To make the dressing into a dip for a dish such as chicken wings (page 128), reduce the amount of dairy kefir to ½ cup (120 milliliters) and add ¼ cup (60 milliliters) Kefir Cream Cheese (page 40), Greek Yogurt (page 37), or sour cream.

SUSHI BAR-STYLE SALAD

FEATURED FERMENTS: **MISO, TAMARI, APPLE CIDER VINEGAR, PICKLED CARROTS**

———

Serves 4

This is my version of the ever-popular salad tossed with bright orange–colored dressing you'll find at many Japanese restaurants, with miso, tamari, cider vinegar, and pickled ginger to bring it alive and romaine lettuce instead of the standard iceberg.

DRESSING
(MAKES ABOUT 1 1/2 CUPS/360 MILLILITERS)

1 large carrot, chopped

3 (3-inch/7.5-centimeter) strips pickled ginger

1 shallot, chopped

1 garlic clove, cut in half

1/4 cup (60 milliliters) raw apple cider vinegar, or to taste

1 tablespoon unpasteurized honey

2 tablespoons light miso, or to taste

2 teaspoons tamari

1/2 cup (120 milliliters) unrefined sesame oil or extra-virgin olive oil

SALAD

1 head romaine or other crisp lettuce, torn into pieces

1 cucumber, sliced

2 radishes, sliced

Large spoonful of shredded pickled carrots (page 32), or 1 large fresh carrot, shredded

Toasted sesame seeds

Make the dressing: In a blender, combine all the ingredients, except the sesame oil, with 2 tablespoons water and blend until smooth. With the machine still running, slowly add the sesame oil through the hole in the lid and blend until emulsified, adding a little more water or oil if the dressing is too thick. Taste and add more miso and/or vinegar if needed.

Make the salad: In a large bowl, combine the lettuce, cucumber, radishes, and carrots and toss. Add dressing to coat (you will have leftover dressing) and toss. Serve immediately.

KALE AND BEET SALAD

FEATURED FERMENTS: **SAUERKRAUT, MISO**

———

Serves 4

Once-humble kale now enjoys superstar veggie status, and kale in the raw makes the base for a hearty, satisfying salad; a quick massage and a toss with a delicious dressing is all that's needed to get it salad ready, and pickled vegetables add extra excitement to this dish. Miso lends its slightly sweet umami flavor to the dressing, honey and a little white wine play off the sweetness, and lemon juice brings all the flavors together. In addition to its standard role as dressing, you can drizzle some over grains or noodles (try it on zucchini noodles; page 133) or stir it into tonight's roasted chicken leftovers for chicken salad sandwiches to bring to work tomorrow. Omit the water and it's a dip for crudités.

SWEET LEMON AND MISO TAHINI DRESSING
(MAKES ABOUT 1¼ CUPS/300 MILLILITERS)

¼ cup (60 milliliters) fresh lemon juice, or to taste

¼ cup (60 milliliters) raw or roasted tahini

¼ cup (60 milliliters) extra-virgin olive oil

2 tablespoons mirin or white wine

2 tablespoons unpasteurized honey

2 tablespoons light miso

¼ teaspoon freshly ground black pepper

Fine sea salt, if needed

SALAD

1 bunch lacinato kale, stems removed, leaves torn into pieces or sliced

2 beets, including greens, greens torn or sliced, roots peeled and coarsely grated

Fine sea salt

¼ to ½ cup (40 to 80 grams) drained sauerkraut, homemade (page 23) or store-bought

1 ripe avocado, halved, pitted, flesh scooped out and chopped

Fresh lemon juice, if needed

¼ cup (35 grams) toasted hulled pumpkin seeds or raw hemp seeds

Make the dressing: In a blender, combine all the ingredients, except the salt, with ¼ cup (60 milliliters) water and blend until smooth, adding a little more water or oil if it's too thick (you want a fairly thin, pourable consistency so it will evenly coat the kale). Taste and add salt and/or more lemon juice if needed.

Make the salad: Put the kale and beet greens in a large bowl; add a large pinch of salt and massage the greens for about a minute, until they start to wilt. Add the grated beets and sauerkraut and toss. Add dressing to coat and massage some dressing into the salad (you will have leftover dressing) to further wilt the greens, then fold in the avocado. Taste and adjust the seasonings with lemon juice and/or salt if needed. Serve topped with the pumpkin seeds and extra dressing alongside for drizzling.

SWAP: Use Cucumber Pickles (page 28), or grated pickled root vegetables (page 32), instead of sauerkraut.

SUPERCHARGE: Use the juiced-up beets from making Beet Kvass (page 61) instead of raw beets.

DILLIED POTATO SALAD

FEATURED FERMENTS: **DILLY BEANS, CULTURED MAYONNAISE**
SUPPORTING FERMENT: **JUICED-UP MUSTARD**

———

Serves 6

This interpretation of the classic potato salad takes picnic food from the predictable to cutting edge. Further elevate your outdoor-meal offerings by packing up some Old-School Apple-Cabbage Slaw (opposite) and Italian-Style Pasta Salad with Giardiniera Sauce (page 123) for your blanket spread, coating your bread with Juiced-up Mustard (page 73) or Wake-up Ketchup (page 74), bringing along a jar of real Cucumber Pickles (page 28), or swapping some Cultured Mayonnaise (page 82) for the supermarket kind in any creamy salad recipe. It's a new way of thinking picnic!

2 pounds (950 grams) boiling (waxy) potatoes

Fine sea salt

¼ cup (60 milliliters) pickling liquid from Dilly Beans (see page 29), plus more if needed

2 teaspoons Juiced-up Mustard

⅔ cup (160 milliliters) Cultured Mayonnaise

1 cup (120 grams) thinly sliced Dilly Beans (page 29)

1 stalk celery, minced

2 shallots, minced

¼ cup (10 grams) finely chopped fresh dill

Coarsely ground black pepper

Put the potatoes in a large pot, add salted cold water to cover by a couple of inches, place over high heat, and bring to a boil. Reduce the heat and simmer, uncovered, until the potatoes are just tender when pierced with a knife, 15 to 25 minutes depending on the size of the potatoes.

Put the pickling liquid in a large bowl and have it ready. Drain the potatoes and peel them when they are just cool enough to handle. Cut the potatoes into bite-size pieces; as you cut each one, immediately add it to the pickling liquid and toss so the liquid is absorbed by the warm potatoes. Stir the mustard and mayonnaise into the still-warm potatoes, then stir in the dilly beans, celery, shallots, and dill. Season generously with pepper, taste, and add some salt or additional pickling liquid if needed.

Serve at room temperature or cold, picnic-style.

SWAP: Substitute chopped dill pickles (page 28) for the Dilly Beans for a more traditional take on the salad.

OLD-SCHOOL APPLE CABBAGE SLAW

FEATURED FERMENTS: **SAUERKRAUT, CULTURED MAYONNAISE**
SUPPORTING FERMENTS: **APPLE CIDER VINEGAR, JUICED-UP MUSTARD**

———————

Makes about 1 quart (1 liter)

This slaw, anointed with a foursome of ferments, is the real deal, passing on the fashionably light vinegar dressing for good old-fashioned mayonnaise, appropriately paired with cold-weather apples and cabbage for its comfort food appeal. And it's not just any mayonnaise—you'll be using farm-fresh eggs to make yours and then culturing it, turning this supermarket staple into a superfood.

DRESSING

½ cup (120 milliliters) Cultured Mayonnaise (page 82)

1 tablespoon raw apple cider vinegar

1 tablespoon Juiced-up Mustard (page 73)

2 tablespoons unpasteurized honey

¼ teaspoon fine sea salt

¼ teaspoon freshly ground black pepper

SLAW

⅓ cup (50 grams) raisins

½ small red cabbage, cored and thinly sliced (about 3 cups/200 grams)

1½ cups (450 grams) drained sauerkraut, homemade (page 23) or store-bought

2 large carrots, peeled and cut into matchsticks

½ cup (40 grams) thinly sliced scallions, white and green parts

2 large apples

2 tablespoons chopped fresh flat-leaf parsley

Salt or sauerkraut juice and freshly ground black pepper, if needed

Make the dressing: In a medium bowl, combine all the ingredients and whisk until homogenous.

Make the slaw: Toss the raisins into the dressing to get them plump and juicy while you do your prep.

In a large bowl, combine the red cabbage, sauerkraut, carrots, and scallions. Add the dressing and stir to coat the vegetables well. Peel 1 apple, core it, and cut it into matchsticks; toss the apple into the slaw as you slice it to prevent browning. Repeat with the second apple. Stir in the parsley, taste, and add some salt or sauerkraut brine and pepper if needed.

TIP: A sprinkling of chopped fermented carrots, turnips, or other vegetables will completely transform any salad.

Local Greens All Year Long

While more and more small-scale farmers are using new and traditional methods to extend the growing season of leafy greens like kale, eating green while staying local still can get pretty tricky come midwinter. That's why we have cabbage: Before refrigeration, cabbage fermented into sauerkraut kept many Europeans stocked with vegetables throughout long winters, and British explorer James Cook was reported to have brought sauerkraut on his long sea voyages to prevent scurvy. In Korea going back to somewhere around the seventh century, cabbage would be buried underground for months to ferment and then unearthed. With a little planning and a lot of cabbage, we can easily have our greens while still eating close to home.

POSEIDON SALAD

FEATURED FERMENTS: CUCUMBER PICKLES, PICKLE JUICE, JUICED-UP MUSTARD, ALL-AROUND ALMOND CHEESE

————

Serves 4 to 6

A unique marriage of the classic Greek and Caesar salads.

MUSTARD AND PICKLE JUICE DRESSING
(MAKES ABOUT 1/2 CUP/120 MILLILITERS)

1/4 cup (60 milliliters) pickle juice (page 29)

1/4 cup (60 milliliters) extra-virgin olive oil

1 tablespoon Juiced-up Mustard (page 73)

1 tablespoon fresh lemon juice

2 tablespoons dulse seaweed flakes

1/4 teaspoon freshly ground black pepper

SALAD

1 head romaine lettuce, torn into pieces

1 cucumber, peeled, seeded, and chopped

1/2 red onion, thinly sliced

1/2 cup (14 grams) packed dulse seaweed fronds, ripped into bite-size pieces

1 nori seaweed sheet, ripped into bite-size pieces

3/4 cup (200 grams) chopped cucumber pickle, homemade (page 28) or store-bought

1/2 cup (100 grams) All-Around Almond Cheese (page 84), crumbled

Fresh lemon juice and fine sea salt, if needed

Make the dressing: Combine all the ingredients in a jar, cover, and shake until the dressing is emulsified.

Make the salad: Combine lettuce, cucumber, onion, dulse, nori, and pickle in a large bowl and toss to combine. Toss with some of the dressing to coat lightly (you will have some leftover dressing). Add the cheese and toss to distribute it among the vegetables. Taste and adjust the seasonings with lemon juice and salt if needed. Serve immediately.

SWAPS: Use Creamy Cashew Cheese (page 83) instead of All-Around Almond Cheese or use a store-bought cultured nut cheese. Those who enjoy dairy could sub feta.

CAULIFLOWER AND RAISIN SALAD
WITH SAFFRON-SCENTED LEMON DRESSING

FEATURED FERMENTS: PRESERVED LEMON, COCONUT WATER KEFIR

Serves 4

Cauliflower in the raw is a powerfully healthful food, most noted for its antioxidant and anticancer properties. Though a raw foods–focused diet is not something that I strive for (except when it comes to ferments, many of which are raw by nature), I try to regularly include some uncooked cauliflower in my diet. Slicing or chopping the cauliflower finely or pulsing florets in a food processor and marinating them is the route to deliciousness for raw cauliflower, and raisins plumped in Coconut Water Kefir add an element of bubbly sweetness to this superfood side salad that matches nicely with a Middle Eastern–themed entrée.

If you come upon cheddar cauliflower at the market, you'll get points for presentation using it here; its beautiful orange color is heightened against the saffron-hued lemon dressing. You'll only need half of the dressing for this recipe; use the rest for salads throughout the week or scale up the cauliflower salad for a double recipe. If you don't have kefir on hand for soaking the raisins, plain coconut water or even plain water is fine.

SALAD

1/2 cup (70 grams) raisins

1/2 cup (120 milliliters) Coconut Water Kefir (page 41) or Water Kefir (page 42)

1 medium head cauliflower, very thinly sliced or finely chopped, either by hand or by pulsing it in a food processor

1/2 bulb fennel, very thinly sliced or coarsely grated (save the tops for Honey-Pickled Fennel, page 182)

1/4 cup (30 grams) pine nuts, toasted

2 tablespoons minced Preserved Lemon peel (page 100)

Handful of fresh mint leaves, chopped

Sea salt and freshly ground black pepper

DRESSING
(MAKES ABOUT 1 CUP/240 MILLILITERS)

1/2 teaspoon saffron threads

1 tablespoon hot water

1 tablespoon fresh lemon juice, or to taste

1/2 Preserved Lemon (page 100), rinsed of excess salt, pulp and seeds removed, peel chopped

1/4 teaspoon ground turmeric

1/2 cup (120 milliliters) extra-virgin olive oil

Fine sea salt to taste

Start the salad: Put the raisins in a small bowl, add the kefir, and set aside to soak for 1 hour. Drain, reserving the kefir for the dressing. Combine the cauliflower, fennel, and raisins in a large bowl.

Make the dressing: Crumble the saffron between two fingers into a small bowl. Add the hot water and leave to "bloom" for 15 minutes (see Note). Pour into a blender, add the lemon juice, the reserved kefir from soaking the raisins, the preserved lemon, and turmeric and blend until smooth. With the motor running, drizzle the oil in through the hole in the lid until the dressing is emulsified. Taste and adjust the seasonings with lemon juice and salt if needed.

Assemble the salad: Add about half of the dressing to the cauliflower mixture and toss to coat very well (you can use your hands to massage the mixture so it coats the cauliflower completely). Add the pine nuts, preserved lemon, and mint and toss to coat. Taste and season with salt, if needed, and plenty of pepper. Leave to marinate for 1 hour at room temperature before serving, or cover and marinate overnight in the refrigerator to allow the lemony flavor to come out to its fullest. The salad will keep, refrigerated, for up to 4 days.

NOTE: Soaking is the best way to extract flavor from saffron, and since saffron is a luxury spice, it pays to make the most of small amounts.

SHORTCUT: Use store-bought preserved lemons, found in glass jars in Middle Eastern food markets. Making your own is a simple process, but curing time is 30 days, making preserved lemons a definite plan-ahead culture!

PRESERVED LEMONS
Makes 5 to 8 preserved lemons

Many Moroccan and Middle Eastern recipes call for preserved lemons, lemons that have been fermented in salt and their own juices for a month. The resulting lemon is salty and intensely lemony yet mellowed of much of the tartness found in fresh lemons.

Minced preserved lemon peel (pulp and seeds generally are removed) is added directly to salads, dressings, dips, stews (see the recipe for Moroccan-Style Lamb Stew with Prunes and Preserved Lemon on page 156), seafood dishes, and even mixed drinks (try a little in the Pickle Mary on page 63); a small amount is all you need to elevate a dish. Try using Meyer lemons if they are available; this sweeter and thinner-skinned variety of lemon takes to salt preservation particularly well. Since you will be eating the peel, make sure your lemons are organic to avoid ingesting chemical sprays.

4 tablespoons fine sea salt

5 to 8 organic unwaxed lemons, scrubbed well and dried

Optional seasonings: dried chile, bay leaf, cinnamon stick, fresh rosemary or thyme sprig, coriander seeds

Fresh lemon juice, if needed

Sprinkle 1 tablespoon of the salt in the bottom of a 1-quart (1-liter) glass jar with a tight-fitting lid. Trim off the little rounded part at the stem end of 5 or 6 lemons and quarter the lemons from the top to within 1/2 inch (12 millimeters) of the bottom (without cutting all the way through) to make an X-shaped incision into the lemons. Pack the remaining 3 tablespoons salt into the exposed flesh, then reshape the fruit.

Pack the lemons into the jar vertically side by side and push them down to release their juices and to make room for all the lemons, leaving at least 1 inch (2.5 centimeters) of space remaining at the top. Add any seasonings you like. Put the lid on the jar and cover tightly. The next day, open the jar and press down on the lemons again so they can release more juice as they soften. Do this again for another day or two. The goal is for the lemons to be completely covered in liquid; if this hasn't happened at this point, add enough fresh lemon juice to submerge the lemons, making sure there is always at least 1 inch (2.5 centimeters) of space at the top. If you find your lemons have shrunk down enough so that they are floating and there's room in the jar to fit another lemon or two, cut and salt them as above and pack them into the jar; you might need to add more lemon juice to cover.

Leave the lemons tightly sealed in a cool spot away from sunlight for 1 month (I like to set a reminder on my calendar). Transfer to the refrigerator, where they will keep for up to a year.

TIP: The pickling juice can be used two or three times more for new batches of preserved lemons or as a flavoring in your recipes; try it in a salad dressing in a three-to-one ratio of olive oil to pickling juice.

PICKLE SALAD TWO WAYS

There are endless ways of making pickles into salad, and when you go beyond the standard dill (see page 29 for suggestions), an infinite number of variations are possible. Here are two to get you started.

ASIAN-STYLE PICKLE SALAD
FEATURED FERMENT: **CUCUMBER PICKLES**
SUPPORTING FERMENT: **FISH SAUCE**
Makes about 1 cup (250 grams)

This salad is intensely flavored and best served in small portions alongside a meal, or you could chop the pickles and onions instead of slicing them and serve as a relish for hamburgers, hotdogs, or the like. Vegetarians can substitute a small amount of tamari for the fish sauce.

1½ cups (400 grams) sliced Cucumber Pickles (page 28; about 2)

½ small red onion, thinly sliced into half-moons

1 tablespoon fish sauce

1 tablespoon extra-virgin olive oil

½ teaspoon toasted sesame oil

2 teaspoons unrefined brown sugar

1 garlic clove, pressed through a garlic press

Pinch of red chile flakes

1 tablespoon chopped fresh mint or cilantro

In a medium bowl, combine the pickles and onion. In a separate bowl, combine the fish sauce, olive oil, sesame oil, brown sugar, garlic, and chile flakes and whisk to dissolve the brown sugar. Pour the dressing over the pickles and toss to coat. Stir in the mint. Serve immediately, or cover and place the salad in the refrigerator, where it will happily marinate until you are ready to serve.

HERBED CUCUMBER AND PICKLE SALAD
FEATURED FERMENT: **CUCUMBER PICKLES**
Serves 4

A perfect balance between fresh and fermented.

3 Cucumber Pickles (page 28), chopped, plus some pickle juice, if needed

3 fresh kirby or pickling cucumbers, chopped

1 large tomato, cored and chopped

2½ tablespoons extra-virgin olive oil

1½ tablespoons chopped fresh flat-leaf parsley

1½ tablespoons chopped fresh dill or other herb of choice

Freshly ground black pepper to taste

Fresh lemon juice (optional)

In a small bowl, combine all the ingredients. Add some pickle juice if more acidity or salt is called for. If the salad is looking for a little brightness but not more salt, add a bit of lemon juice.

CHAPTER FIVE

SOUPS

BASIC MISO SOUP
WITH ENDLESS VARIATIONS

FEATURED FERMENT: **MISO**

———————

Serves 4 to 6

Every fan of fermentation should have a good miso soup recipe under her belt, and not the kind that comes from opening a packet and stirring it into hot water (a classic example of a live food turned dead). Traditional miso soup is made from a dashi stock based on bonito (dried fish flakes) and kombu, a sea vegetable that boosts flavor and nutrient content without adding a seaweed flavor. Both can be found in Japanese groceries and natural food stores. Your from-scratch miso soup will be brimming with umami, especially when an authentic brand such as South River is used. Red miso is stronger than mellow white, so start with a lesser amount when using red.

1 piece kombu seaweed (about 3 by 4 inches/7.5 by 10 centimeters)

1½ cups (8 grams) bonito flakes (omit for vegetarians)

6 to 8 tablespoons white, red, or other miso paste

¼ cup (½ ounce/14 grams) dried wakame seaweed (optional)

8 shiitake mushrooms, thinly sliced (optional)

1 teaspoon toasted sesame oil (optional)

4 scallions, white and green parts, thinly sliced (optional)

Combine 6 cups (1½ liters) water, the kombu, and bonito in a large saucepan. Place over medium-high heat and bring just to a boil. Turn off the heat, cover, and leave for 5 minutes. Uncover, then strain through a fine-mesh strainer into a new pan; discard the solids. Rinse the strainer and lower it into the broth. Add the miso paste to the strainer and, using the back of a spoon, press the paste through the strainer into the broth, discarding the large grains that don't pass through. Add the wakame and mushrooms, if using. Garnish with the sesame oil and scallions, if you like, and serve immediately.

SWAP: Use Traditional Broth (page 108) or Vegetable Broth (page 109) instead of bonito broth if that's what you have on hand.

SUPERCHARGE: Add a little pickle juice (page 29) or kimchi juice (page 25) after the soup comes off the burner to up your culture and add a burst of flavor.

VARIATIONS

As the recipe title indicates, the add-in options are endless. Here are a few ideas to get you started:

- Silken or cubed firm tofu, a drizzle of tamari, and sesame seeds
- Blanched carrot, daikon, and turnip
- Braised sweet potato and fresh spinach leaves
- Roasted kabocha squash and toasted sesame seeds
- Rice, hard-boiled egg, and pickle
- Potato and sautéed leek
- Salmon and 100 percent buckwheat soba noodles
- Onions, cabbage, shrimp (add them directly to the soup to steam), and a dash of hot sauce
- Shredded cooked chicken, rice, and ginger
- Thin slices of beef, baby bok choy (add them directly to the soup to quickly cook), and toasted sesame oil

QUINOA SWEET POTATO CONGEE
WITH JAPANESE SALTED PLUMS

FEATURED FERMENTS: **FERMENTED QUINOA, UMEBOSHI PLUMS**

———

Serves 4 to 6

Congee is a porridgelike soup eaten throughout Asia, typically for breakfast. Classic congee is based on rice, cooked very slowly in abundant broth, making it an easy-to-digest, nourishing, and soul-satisfying food. Here I've used quinoa instead of the rice and fermented it before cooking to further heighten its health profile. (For more on fermenting grains, see page 49.) The dish's uncooked ferment is the Japanese umeboshi plum; its salty-tart taste adds a bright note to this otherwise earthy soup. For a vegan version, omit the chicken and use vegetable stock or water as the soup base.

1 cup (200 grams) quinoa, rinsed well

2 tablespoons raw apple cider vinegar

2 quarts (2 liters) Traditional Broth (page 108) or Vegetable Broth (page 109) or water

1 large sweet potato, peeled and chopped

4 dates, pitted and chopped

One 2-inch (5-centimeter) piece kombu seaweed

1 bay leaf

1¹/2 teaspoons fine sea salt

¹/2 teaspoon freshly ground black pepper

1 ripe plantain, peeled and chopped (optional)

1 chicken leg (optional)

¹/2 cup (70 grams) raw peanuts or cashews (optional)

1 to 2 dried red chiles (optional)

Extra-virgin olive oil

6 umeboshi plums, pitted and finely chopped

Put the quinoa in a large bowl and rinse until the water runs clear, then drain. Add the vinegar and 3 cups (720 milliliters) water. Cover with a clean dish towel and soak for 1 to 2 days, depending on the season and kitchen temperature. It will be ready when it smells just slightly fermented; it won't change all that much. Drain and rinse until the water runs clear.

Put the quinoa in a large saucepan. Add the broth, sweet potato, dates, kombu, bay leaf, salt, pepper, and, if you wish, the plantain, chicken, peanuts, and/or chile (a single chile can add a fair amount of heat when it cooks for a long time). Bring to a boil over medium-high heat, then reduce the heat to very low so it's at a bare simmer (a flame tamer or heat diffuser, a metal disk designed to decrease the amount of heat coming from the stove to the pan, works well here) and cook for at least 3 hours or up to 8 hours, adding more broth or water if needed. (Alternatively, cook your congee in a slow cooker on low for about 8 hours.)

Remove the kombu and bay leaf. Remove the chicken if you used it, shred it if it hasn't already fallen off the bone, discard the bone, and return the meat to the pan. Crush the sweet potatoes with a potato masher if they haven't already dissolved into the soup. Adjust the seasonings and serve, with each bowl topped with a drizzle of oil and some of the umeboshi plum.

SWAPS: Substitute finely chopped Preserved Lemon (page 100) for the umeboshi. Umeboshi paste or a simple splash of umeboshi vinegar could also be used.

Use millet instead of quinoa or use half quinoa and half millet.

BUTTERNUT SQUASH, SAUERKRAUT, AND HOT SAUSAGE SOUP

FEATURED FERMENT: **SAUERKRAUT**

———————

Serves 6 to 8

Sauerkraut soup is a dish with eastern European roots, a hearty cold-weather soup making use of ingredients that have been preserved for winter use. I've added squash to keep with the wintry theme, along with warming coriander, cinnamon, nutmeg, and cloves—and hot Italian sausage for extra thermal effects. You could use any other type of winter squash in place of the butternut, if you like; delicata and red or green kuri make excellent choices.

3 tablespoons extra-virgin olive oil, plus more if needed

12 ounces (340 grams) hot Italian sausage (3 sausages), sliced 1/2 inch (12 millimeters) thick

2 leeks, white and light green parts, chopped

2 garlic cloves, chopped

1 teaspoon sweet paprika

3/4 teaspoon ground coriander

3/4 teaspoon ground cinnamon

3/4 teaspoon freshly grated nutmeg

Pinch of ground cloves

1 small butternut squash, halved, peeled, seeded, and chopped (about 4 cups)

Splash of white wine (optional)

6 cups (1.5 liters) Traditional Broth (page 108) or Vegetable Broth (page 109)

Fine sea salt

2 cups (300 grams) chopped sauerkraut, homemade (page 23) or store-bought, with brine, plus more brine if needed

Fresh lemon juice if needed

1 tablespoon minced fresh flat-leaf parsley

In a large saucepan, heat the oil over medium heat. Add the sausage and brown it, about 5 minutes on each side. Using a slotted spoon, remove the sausage from the pan and put it on a plate. Add the leeks to the fat in the pan (add a little oil if the pan looks dry) and cook for about 5 minutes, until softened. Add the garlic and cook for another 2 minutes or so, until softened. Add the paprika, coriander, cinnamon, nutmeg, and cloves and cook for about 1 minute, stirring, until the spices are aromatic. Add the squash and sauté for about 2 minutes, until well coated with the spices. Add the wine, if using (if you're not using wine, add a splash of the broth), and stir to release any browned bits from the bottom of the pan.

Add the broth and a pinch of salt. Increase the heat to medium-high, partially cover, and bring to a boil. Reduce the heat to low and simmer for about 30 minutes, until the squash has softened.

Coarsely mash some of the squash with a potato masher, turn off the heat, uncover the pan, and leave it for 5 minutes, then stir in the sauerkraut. Taste and add a little sauerkraut brine or salt if needed; if you'd like a little extra brightness without salting the soup, add a splash of lemon juice. Stir in the parsley and serve.

SWAP: To turn the soup vegetarian, omit the sausage, use vegetable broth, and add cayenne to taste to give the soup some heat.

TRADITIONAL BROTH

Makes about 3½ quarts (3.5 liters)

Many of us who are attracted to traditional foods have discovered the nourishing qualities of old-fashioned broth based on chicken, beef, pork, or other animal bones and use it freely as an elevated ingredient in our cooking. The reasons to make your own are many: First, the rich, rounded flavors of traditional broth give a noticeable upgrade to any recipe that you use it in. Second, broth is a deeply healing food and a nutritional powerhouse, offering a host of easily absorbable minerals including calcium, magnesium, and phosphorus, and it is anti-inflammatory. Third, it's economical, as it makes use of bones you otherwise would have thrown away. Finally, it supports and heals the digestive tract, making it a powerful partner to probiotic-rich ferments.

Don't think of this as a hard and fast recipe but rather a guideline to get you started. Once you've got a groove you'll see that it's hard to go wrong: It's little more than tossing some bones and flavoring ingredients into a pot with water to cover and simmering away.

2 to 3 pounds (900 grams to 1.4 kilograms) pastured chicken, beef, pork, or other animal bones (see Note)

4 quarts (4 liters) cold filtered water

Optional vegetables: 2 carrots, roughly chopped; 1 large onion, quartered; 2 celery stalks, roughly chopped; and/or 2 garlic cloves, peeled

2 bay leaves (optional)

1 piece kombu seaweed (about 3 by 4 inches/7.5 by 10 centimeters; see Note), lightly rinsed

2 tablespoons raw apple cider vinegar (see Note)

1 teaspoon fine sea salt, or to taste (optional; see Note)

Place the bones in a large stockpot. Add the water and bring just to a boil; boil for 5 minutes, skimming any foam from the top. Add the vegetables and bay leaves, if using, kombu, vinegar, and salt. Cover, reduce the heat to very low, and cook at a bare simmer for 12 hours. Alternatively, combine all the ingredients in a slow cooker, turn it to low, and cook for 12 to 24 hours.

Remove the bones with tongs or a slotted spoon, then strain the broth through a fine-mesh strainer lined with cheesecloth into a heatproof bowl. Use immediately, or cool, pour into containers, and store in the refrigerator for up to 1 week or the freezer for up to 3 months.

NOTES: Tossing the carcass from tonight's roasted chicken into a pot is a simple way to start a stock.

Kombu is a mineral-rich sea vegetable; it adds even more nutrients to your broth and enhances its savory (umami) flavor, as it is based on glutamic acid, nature's version of MSG. The seaweed strips often are coated in a white powder that comes from natural salts; this can be removed with a light rinse.

Vinegar helps extract the minerals from the bones and into your broth.

Salt helps to bring out flavor in the stock but is not required; adjust the amount up or down depending on the recipes you plan to use it in.

VEGETABLE BROTH

Makes 3 quarts (3 liters)

Vegetable broth boasts a host of minerals, extracting the essence from your veggies with a bonus of mineral-rich kombu seaweed. Vegetable broth is ready in under an hour and is worlds above anything you'll buy in a can or box.

Use my measurements as a guideline and feel free to swap in just about any vegetables you like, avoiding cabbage family members for their overly pungent flavor and using vegetables that match the dish they are going in, such as corncobs and corn husks for the summer chowder on page 112 or winter squash skins and seeds for the butternut squash soup on page 107.

2 tablespoons extra-virgin olive oil

2 large onions, roughly chopped

3 large carrots, roughly chopped

2 large celery stalks, including leaves, roughly chopped

4 garlic cloves, smashed (include the peels)

2 handfuls of parsley stems or sprigs

2 bay leaves

1 or 2 pieces kombu seaweed (about 3 by 4 inches/7.5 by 10 centimeters each; see Note, opposite), lightly rinsed

1 teaspoon fine sea salt, or to taste (optional; see Note opposite)

1 teaspoon whole black peppercorns

3 quarts (3 liters) cold filtered water

Heat the oil in a large stockpot over medium-high heat. Add the onions, carrots, celery, and garlic and cook, stirring frequently, until well browned, about 10 minutes. Add the remaining ingredients and bring to a boil. Reduce the heat to very low, cover, and cook at a bare simmer for 45 minutes. Strain the broth through a fine-mesh strainer into a heatproof bowl. Use immediately, or cool, pour into containers, and store in the refrigerator for up to 1 week or the freezer for up to 3 months.

SUPERCHARGE: Add a handful or two of fresh shiitake stems or whole dried shiitake mushrooms (soak dried shiitakes in water to cover for 30 minutes first); they will increase the savory flavor of your stock while detoxifying your body and boosting your immunity.

NOTE: Save vegetable scraps in a plastic bag or container in the freezer. When there's enough to fill a pot halfway, throw them in, add a piece or two of kombu and some salt, pour in water to cover, and proceed as above.

POLISH-STYLE COLD BEET SOUP

FEATURED FERMENTS: **DAIRY YOGURT, GREEK YOGURT, CUCUMBER PICKLES, PICKLE JUICE**

Serves 4 to 6

The name for this soup in Polish is *chłodnik*, which translates to "cooling," and this classic cold beet soup is just that, a counterpart to its Russian hot borscht cousin. It has the cooling properties of gazpacho, but its hearty ingredients make this a summer meal in a bowl, crossing the boundary between soup and salad. Traditionally young spring or summer beets are used for the tastiest soup.

4 large beets, scrubbed, stems removed and reserved, greens chopped and reserved

2 medium to large cucumbers, peeled, seeded, and diced or coarsely grated

4 radishes, diced or coarsely grated

2 garlic cloves, pressed through a garlic press

1 cup (240 milliliters) yogurt, homemade (page 34) or store-bought

¼ cup (60 milliliters) Greek yogurt, homemade (page 37) or store-bought, plus more for garnish if you like

About 1½ cups (360 milliliters) pickle juice (page 29)

Juice of 1 lemon, or to taste

2 large handfuls of fresh dill, chopped, plus more for garnish if you like

Fine sea salt

1 cucumber or young zucchini pickle (page 28), diced (optional)

2 hard-boiled eggs, diced (optional)

Bring a large saucepan of water to a boil. Add the beets and stems, return to a boil, then cover partially and simmer for about 45 minutes, until a knife easily pierces a beet all the way through. Remove the beets and stems from the water and set the liquid aside for later use. Discard the stems, or finely chop them and save them to add to the soup when you add the greens. Cool the beets for a few minutes, then peel them with your fingers; the skin should slip off easily. (Wear disposable gloves while working with beets if you prefer not to color your hands.)

Finely mince or coarsely grate the beets and put them in a large bowl. Add the cucumbers, radishes, garlic, regular and Greek yogurts, pickle juice, lemon juice, and dill and stir to combine. Add reserved beet cooking water to thin the soup to your liking, about 1 cup (240 milliliters), keeping the soup fairly thick. Taste and season with salt, the amount depending on how salty your pickle juice is, and add more lemon juice if needed. Stir in the reserved beet greens and the stems, if using. Cover and refrigerate for at least 4 hours or overnight. Taste and adjust the seasonings if needed. Serve cold, garnished with some Greek yogurt, dill, pickle, and the hard-boiled eggs if you like.

SWAPS: Use sauerkraut brine or any other pickling brine instead of the pickle juice.

Substitute Beet Kvass (page 61) for some or all of the pickle juice.

Substitute Kefir Cream Cheese (page 40) or Countertop Crème Fraîche (page 79) for the Greek yogurt.

To make a dairy- and egg-free beet soup, use Coconut Milk Kefir (page 41) or Young Coconut Yogurt (page 37) instead of the dairy yogurt and top with diced avocado in place of the hard-boiled egg.

SUMMER CHOWDER

FEATURED FERMENTS: **CUCUMBER PICKLES, PICKLE JUICE, GREEK YOGURT**

Serves 6

Pickle soup is popular in Polish and Russian cuisine; it's a hearty dish often thickened with sour cream. I've turned my pickle soup into a warm-weather potato-and-corn–based chowder and thicken it with yogurt instead of sour cream to keep it summery light. I've stuck to basic seasonings so you can include whatever flavor of pickles you've got going in the fermentation jar (see page 29 for ideas) at any given time. When I'm making this soup with standard dill pickles, I like to include a tablespoon of ground caraway seeds; I add them just after the garlic is cooked, stirring for a minute or so until aromatic, and then finish the soup with a little fresh dill. The soup can be served warm, at room temperature, or chilled.

2 tablespoons extra-virgin olive oil

1 onion, chopped

2 garlic cloves, finely chopped

1 quart (1 liter) Traditional Broth (page 108) or Vegetable Broth (page 109), plus more if needed

Fine sea salt

1 pound (450 grams) potatoes, peeled and cut into 1/2-inch (1.25-centimeter) cubes

2 carrots, chopped

2 celery stalks, chopped

Kernels from 2 ears corn (about 1 1/2 cups/240 grams)

1 1/2 cups (360 milliliters) Greek yogurt, homemade (page 37) or store-bought, plus more for serving

1 cup (300 grams) diced Cucumber Pickles (page 28)

3/4 cup (180 milliliters) pickle juice (page 29), or to taste

Freshly ground black pepper

Fresh lemon juice, if needed

1/4 cup (10 grams) chopped fresh dill or flat-leaf parsley

In a large saucepan, heat the oil over medium heat. Add the onion and cook until softened, about 5 minutes. Add the garlic and cook for about 2 minutes, until softened. Add the broth and a pinch of salt, cover, bring to a boil, then add the potatoes, carrots, and celery, partially cover, and cook until the vegetables are softened, about 15 minutes. Add the corn and cook for about 2 minutes, until softened. Remove from the heat and leave the soup for 5 minutes.

Temper the yogurt by placing it in a medium bowl and slowly whisking in a few ladlefuls of the hot soup. Return the yogurt to the pan, stir or whisk it in well, then stir in the pickles, pickle juice, and tempered yogurt. Transfer 1 quart (1 liter) of the soup from the pan to a blender and blend until smooth, then return it to the pan. Season generously with pepper, then taste your soup. If it's not salty enough, add some more pickle juice (if it's not salty enough but it's at the thickness you like, just add a little salt). Add more broth or water if the soup is too thick. If the dish needs a little brightness without the addition of salt, add a little lemon juice. Add the dill and serve immediately, topped with Greek yogurt, or cool to room temperature, cover, and refrigerate and serve cold.

SWAP: Substitute sauerkraut and sauerkraut brine (page 23) for the pickles and pickle juice. In Poland potatoes and sauerkraut are the basis for the soup known as *kapusniak.*

CHILLED CANTALOUPE AND TARRAGON SOUP

FEATURED FERMENT: **GREEK YOGURT**

———

Serves 4

This light and refreshing melon soup punctuated with sweet anise-like tarragon works equally well as a palate cleanser or cooling afternoon snack. Or serve it for dessert, finished with a dollop of Greek yogurt or lemon ice cream. Note that fruit ferments faster than vegetables, so check your soup a couple of times a day, as it can go from lightly fermented to overfermented in a matter of hours in a hot summer kitchen and continues to ferment a bit after it's refrigerated (signs of possible overfermentation are a strong alcohol smell and taste, very active bubbling, and a mealy appearance).

1 large cantaloupe (about 4 pounds/1.75 kilograms), flesh cut into chunks

1 cucumber, peeled, seeded, and chopped

1/2 cup (120 milliliters) unpasteurized honey

1/2 cup (120 milliliters) fresh lime juice

1/4 cup (60 milliliters) Water Kefir (page 42), liquid whey (page 20), or other starter culture (optional; page 19)

1 teaspoon fine sea salt

1 1/2 tablespoons finely chopped fresh tarragon, plus sprigs for garnishing

1/2 cup (60 milliliters) Greek yogurt, homemade (page 37) or store-bought, plus more for serving if you like

Lemon and Tart Dried Cherry Crème Fraîche Ice Cream (optional; page 172)

Combine the cantaloupe, cucumber, honey, lime juice, Water Kefir, if using, and salt in a blender (you may need to do this in two batches, blending half of the ingredients in each batch) and blend until smooth. Add the tarragon and blend for a few seconds to incorporate it. Transfer to a 2-quart (2-liter) glass jar with a lid. Tighten the lid, then open it a quarter turn. Place it in a high-sided container large enough to fit it with a little room, cover with a dish towel, and set aside away from sunlight for about 24 hours, checking it and stirring it a couple of times. Press through a fine-mesh strainer into a bowl, pressing on the solids to release all the liquid. Discard the solids and stir in the yogurt. Transfer to a container, leaving a couple of inches of space at the top, cover, and refrigerate until cold, about 2 hours. Open the lid slowly over the sink (it's alive, so it might bubble up a bit and cause a little excitement as it is opened). The soup will keep for about 2 days in the refrigerator.

Stir the soup before serving (it most likely will have separated), then spoon into bowls and serve, garnished with tarragon sprigs and a dollop of yogurt or a scoop of ice cream if you like.

SWAP: Substitute Countertop Crème Fraîche (page 79) for the yogurt.

CHAPTER FIVE

STARTERS AND SIDES

GUACAMOLE WITH A KICK

FEATURED FERMENT: **SALSA ALIVE**

Serves 4 to 6

When you have Salsa Alive in the fridge, this guac is almost instant, and it brings your avocados to life. Perfect for impromptu entertaining.

3 ripe Hass avocados

¾ cup (200 grams) Salsa Alive (page 76)

Cut the avocados in half, remove the pits, and scoop the flesh into a large bowl. Smash them with a fork or whisk to your desired texture. Stir in the salsa (if your salsa is on the liquidy side, scoop it out with a slotted spoon) and serve immediately, with crudités, crackers, or chips, atop a salad, or alongside an entrée.

MISOMITE ON TOAST

FEATURED FERMENT: **MISO**

Makes 4 slices

This is a play on the sticky, salty, yeasty spread known as Marmite that's wildly popular in Britain, Australia, and New Zealand and is something people generally love or hate. This version, using miso instead of yeast extract, is easy to love. It also could be served as a dip for chips or used as the base of a creamy dairy-free salad dressing.

1 avocado, halved, pitted, and flesh scooped out

1 tablespoon mellow white miso or dark miso

4 slices toast

Fresh cilantro or flat-leaf parsley leaves

In a medium bowl, combine the avocado and miso and mash with a fork until fairly smooth or totally smooth, however you like it. Spread onto the toast, cut into quarters, top with cilantro leaves, and serve immediately.

MINI CAPRESE SALAD SKEWERS
WITH MISO-MARINATED MOZZARELLA

FEATURED FERMENT: **MISO**

———————

Makes 16 mini skewers

Mild-flavored and soft-textured mozzarella was made for marination; here a miso–white wine infusion adds an element of sweet and umami flavor to this take on the classic Caprese salad. If basil is unavailable, arugula can be substituted. The recipe scales up easily to serve as a passed party app.

1/2 cup (120 grams) light miso

1/4 cup (60 milliliters) mirin (Japanese rice wine) or other white wine

16 bocconcini (small mozzarella cheese balls; about 6 ounces/170 grams)

16 small cherry tomatoes

16 fresh basil leaves

Extra-virgin olive oil

Freshly ground black pepper

In a small bowl, whisk the miso with the mirin to dissolve the miso. Put the bocconcini in a zip-top bag, add the miso marinade, seal the bag, and massage the marinade into the bocconcini. Place in the refrigerator and leave to marinate for 2 to 3 days, massaging the marinade into the bocconcini once a day or when you think of it.

Remove the bocconcini from the marinade, lightly rinse them, and pat dry with paper towels. Skewer a cherry tomato with a cocktail stick. Fold a basil leaf in half and skewer it onto the stick. Finish with a mozzarella ball. Place the skewers on a large plate or small individual serving plates, drizzle with olive oil, and finish with a good grinding of black pepper.

SWAP: For a dairy-free Caprese, swap the mozzarella for almond cheese (page 84), roll it into balls, and skip the marination. Roll the balls in Miso Parmesan (page 85) if you have some on hand. If you have a dehydrator, a couple of hours spent in it at 145°F (62°C) would help to firm them up.

LEMON AND CAPER CREAM CHEESE-STUFFED MUSHROOMS

FEATURED FERMENT: **KEFIR CREAM CHEESE**
SUPPORTING FERMENT: **APPLE CIDER VINEGAR**

———————

Makes 16 stuffed mushrooms

Stuffed mushrooms are classic party food, and variations abound, but I'm guessing a mushroom stuffed with kefir will be a first for most of your guests! Expect them back for seconds. The mushrooms themselves can be brined (see sidebar), giving you another option for stuffing.

16 large white mushrooms (about 1½ pounds), cleaned, stems removed (save the stems for stock)

¼ cup (60 milliliters) extra-virgin olive oil

2 tablespoons raw apple cider vinegar

2 garlic cloves, pressed through a garlic press

1 tablespoon minced fresh rosemary, or 1 teaspoon dried rosemary

Fine sea salt and freshly ground black pepper

½ cup (120 milliliters) Kefir Cream Cheese (page 40)

2 teaspoons finely grated lemon zest

Capers, rinsed, drained, and patted dry

16 small fresh mint leaves

Preheat the oven to 400°F (200°C).

Put the mushrooms in a large bowl. Add the oil, vinegar, garlic, and rosemary, season with salt and pepper, and toss to coat the mushrooms. Place them on a baking sheet, tops facing up, and roast for about 10 minutes, until the mushrooms have softened and released a good amount of liquid but aren't browned. Return them with their cooking liquid to the bowl and cool. Transfer to a jar or bowl, cover, and refrigerate for at least 8 hours or overnight, shaking the jar a few times to disperse the marinade.

Remove the mushrooms from their marinade and dry off excess liquid with paper towels. In a medium bowl, combine the kefir cream cheese and lemon zest and season with salt and pepper. Spoon the cheese into the mushroom caps, using about ½ tablespoon

for each. Top each stuffed mushroom with a couple of capers and a mint leaf, grind some pepper on top, and serve.

SUPERCHARGE: Top your mushrooms with a little minced preserved lemon skin (page 100) or a pinch of minced umeboshi plum in place of the capers.

Brining Mushrooms

To brine mushrooms, pack a glass jar with a lid tightly with your choice of mushrooms. If adding seasonings such as rosemary or thyme sprigs, wedge them among the mushrooms. Pour enough Basic Salt Brine (page 20) over the mushrooms to cover them, leaving at least 1 inch (2.5 centimeters) of space remaining at the top. Place a glass filled with water or a small ramekin with a rock placed in it that fits snugly into your jar and press down on it until the brine rises over the level of the mushrooms.

Place the jar on a rimmed plate to catch any potential overflow, cover with a clean dish towel and set aside in a cool place away from sunlight to ferment. After a few days, check your mushrooms, removing mold if any develops (don't worry if you don't get all of the mold; you've created an anaerobic environment in which it is almost impossible for bad bacteria to take root). Your mushrooms will be ready in about 5 days, depending on the season and kitchen temperature. Remove the weight, cover, and place in the refrigerator, where they will keep for about 2 months.

PINK PICKLED BABY TURNIP CARPACCIO

FEATURED FERMENT: **PINK PICKLED BABY TURNIPS**

Serves 4

While winter turnips typically make their way into cold-weather soups and stews, small, delicate baby turnips are among the first early-season roots that come up for pickling. For this dish I thinly slice the turnip pickles to reveal their rose-petal-pink interior and elegantly arrange them on plates so they can be properly admired before digging in. Save the turnip greens to add to a salad or soup, or chop them and slip them into your next batch of sauerkraut.

4 to 6 Pink Pickled Baby Turnips (see recipe at right)

Extra-virgin olive oil

Coarsely ground black pepper

Parmesan cheese shavings (optional)

Microgreens (optional)

Slice the turnips as thinly as possible using a sharp knife. Arrange the turnips on a large serving plate or 4 individual serving plates. Drizzle generously with oil, grind some pepper on top, and scatter some Parmesan shavings and microgreens on top if you like. Serve immediately.

PINK PICKLED BABY TURNIPS
Makes 1 quart (1 liter)

8 to 10 baby turnips (about 1 ounce/30 grams each), greens removed, ends trimmed, and scrubbed well

2 red beet slices

About 1¾ cups (420 milliliters) Basic Salt Brine (page 20)

Tightly pack the turnips into a 1-quart (1-liter) glass. Nestle in a beet slice or two. Pour enough brine over the turnips to cover them, leaving at least 1 inch (2.5 centimeters) of space remaining at the top.

Choose a weight that fits snugly into your jar (such as a glass filled with water or a small ramekin with a rock in it) and press down on it until the brine rises over the level of the turnips. Place the jar on a rimmed plate (a glass pie plate works nicely) to catch any potential overflow, cover with a clean dish towel, and set aside in a cool place away from sunlight to ferment. After a few days, check your turnips, removing mold if any develops (don't worry if you don't get all of the mold; you've created an anaerobic environment in which it is almost impossible for bad bacteria to take root).

Your turnips will be ready in about 1 week, depending on the season and kitchen temperature and how tangy you like them. Remove the weight, cover, and place in the refrigerator, where they will keep for about 6 months.

CHEESY KIMCHI PANCAKES

FEATURED FERMENT: **KIMCHI**
SUPPORTING FERMENTS: **FISH SAUCE, LIVE AND KICKIN' HOT SAUCE**

———

Makes 3 large pancakes or multiple small pancakes

This is a gluten-free version of the pancakes offered at many Korean restaurants, enriched with mild grated cheese and fortified with fermented cabbage. Fresh uncooked kimchi garnishes the dish and serves as your raw ferment. The amount of fish sauce or salt and hot sauce you need depends on how salty and spicy your kimchi is. After you've made a batch or two with your personal kimchi, you'll get a feel for how much to season. Those who are dairy free can omit the cheese; those who like oozing-with-cheese pancakes can up the amount suggested here.

½ cup (80 grams) white rice flour (see Note)

¼ cup (30 grams) cornstarch or potato starch

½ cup (120 milliliters) kimchi juice (page 25) or water (see Note)

3 large farm-fresh eggs, beaten

2 cups (8 ounces/225 grams) grated Monterey Jack cheese

Fish sauce or salt

Live and Kickin' Hot Sauce (page 81)

2 cups (520 grams) chopped (if pieces are large) kimchi, homemade (page 25) or store-bought, plus more for serving

3 scallions, white and light green parts, finely chopped, plus more for serving

Unrefined virgin coconut oil

Toasted sesame seeds

Heat a 10-inch (25-centimeter) cast-iron skillet over medium heat for at least 5 minutes while you make the pancake batter.

Sift the rice flour and cornstarch into a large bowl, then whisk in the kimchi juice, eggs, and 1¾ cups of the cheese. Season with fish sauce and hot sauce and stir in the kimchi and scallions.

Spoon 2 tablespoons coconut oil into the skillet and tilt the skillet to evenly coat it with oil. Spread one third of the batter over the skillet, using a wooden spoon or spatula to make sure the kimchi is evenly distributed. Cook for about 5 minutes, until the edges are dry and you can easily lift a section of the pancake with a thin metal spatula (and when you lift it the underside is nicely browned). Slide the pancake onto a large, flat plate, cover it with another plate, and flip it. Slide the overturned pancake back into the skillet and cook for about 5 minutes, until the second side is nicely browned.

Loosen the pancake with a spatula and slide it onto a plate. Cover loosely to keep warm while you make two more pancakes. Sprinkle the remaining ¼ cup cheese over the pancakes and top with fresh kimchi, scallions, and sesame seeds. Cut into wedges using a pizza cutter or sharp knife and top with hot sauce if you like.

NOTES: White rice flour is available in Asian markets and some natural food stores and supermarkets; to make your own, simply grind dry white rice in a spice grinder to a fine powder.

If your kimchi jar doesn't yield enough kimchi juice, supplement what you have with water, or pickle juice if you have some on hand.

ITALIAN-STYLE PASTA SALAD
WITH GIARDINIERA SAUCE

FEATURED FERMENT: **GIARDINIERA**

———

Serves 4 to 6

All the highlights of a good Italian antipasto pasta salad, but with a wholesome upgrade, as the pasta skips the gluten, the vegetables are traditionally pickled, and the salami is naturally cured. The giardiniera recipe makes enough for two batches of pasta; it can also be spiced with fresh hot chiles and used as a Chicago-style condiment for sandwiches, hot dogs, and hamburgers.

1 quart (1 liter) Giardiniera (see recipe at right)

8 ounces (225 grams) rice-based shells, spirals, or other pasta shape, cooked

4 ounces (225 grams) fresh mozzarella cheese, cut into cubes

4 ounces (225 grams) naturally cured salami, cut into small cubes

4 thin slices prosciutto, torn into pieces (optional)

1 cup (225 grams) cherry tomatoes, cut in half

¼ cup (60 milliliters) extra-virgin olive oil

3 tablespoons chopped fresh flat-leaf parsley, plus more for sprinkling

Freshly ground black pepper

Fine sea salt if needed

Drain the giardiniera, reserving ⅓ cup (80 milliliters) of the brine (save the remaining pickling brine for another dressing, a soup flavoring, or as a marinade for meat). Put the giardiniera in a large bowl and add the pasta, cheese, salami, prosciutto, and cherry tomatoes.

   In a medium bowl, whisk the oil with the brine. Pour the dressing over the salad and stir to coat. Add the parsley and season with pepper. Taste and add more brine or salt if needed. Spoon into bowls and serve garnished with parsley.

GIARDINIERA
MAKES 2 QUARTS (2 LITERS)

This is the classic Italian condiment, made by salt brining the vegetables instead of the usual pickling in vinegar.

1 small to medium head cauliflower, cut into small florets (about 4 cups)

1 small red bell pepper, cored, seeded, and thinly sliced

1 small yellow or orange bell pepper, cored, seeded, and thinly sliced

1 large carrot, thinly sliced

1 large stalk celery, thinly sliced

6 garlic cloves, thinly sliced

1 tablespoon dried oregano

1 to 2 teaspoons red chile flakes

½ teaspoon celery seeds

About 1½ quarts (1.5 liters) Basic Salt Brine (page 20)

In a large bowl, combine all the ingredients except the brine. Transfer the mixture to a 2-quart (2-liter) jar or crock or two 1-quart (1-liter) jars. Pour enough of the brine over the vegetables to cover them, leaving at least 1 inch (2.5 centimeters) of space remaining at the top. Weight the jars and ferment following the instructions for root vegetables brining (page 32).

PROSCIUTTO-WRAPPED PICKLED ASPARAGUS

FEATURED FERMENT: **PICKLED ASPARAGUS**

This is the perfect make-ahead party food: Have your pickled asparagus spears on hand and it takes just minutes to wrap them, rewarding you with an elegant presentation and a salty, tangy take on the classic app.

16 spears Pickled Asparagus (see recipe below)

16 paper-thin slices prosciutto

Freshly ground black pepper

Remove the asparagus from the brine and pat dry with paper towels. Wrap each spear with a slice of prosciutto. Arrange decoratively on a platter, grind some pepper on top, and serve.

PICKLED ASPARAGUS
Makes 1 quart (1 liter)

This is one of my favorite ferments, hard to stop eating after the first taste; I suggest doubling the asparagus so you'll have some left to snack on, serve on an antipasto platter, or garnish a Pickle Mary (page 63). The asparagus will shrink a bit, so pack it in the jar well. The seasonings here are suggestions; feel free to mix and match with whatever herbs or spices call to you.

1 bunch thin asparagus spears

2 teaspoons coriander seeds

2 teaspoons dill seeds

About 2 cups (480 milliliters) Basic Salt Brine (page 20)

Trim the asparagus of its woody ends (save them for soup stock), then cut them into lengths that fit into a glass 1-quart (1-liter) jar, leaving 1 inch (2.5 centimeters) space at the top (cook any leftovers, toss them into another jar of ferments, or include them with the woody ends for an extra-flavorful soup stock). Lay the jar on its side and stuff the asparagus into the jar. If there's room remaining, wedge in other vegetables such as carrot sticks or turnip slices so there's a tight fit and you'll have some bonus pickled vegetables when fermentation has been completed. Add the coriander and dill seeds. Pour enough brine over the asparagus to cover it, leaving at least 1 inch (2.5 centimeters) of space remaining at the top.

Cover the jar, shake it a few times to disperse the seeds, place it on a rimmed plate (a glass pie plate works nicely) to catch any potential leakage or bubbling over when you open the lid, cover with a clean dish towel to keep out insects, and set aside in a cool place away from sunlight to ferment. After a few days, check your asparagus, removing mold if any develops (don't worry if you don't get all of the mold; you've created an anaerobic environment in which it is almost impossible for bad bacteria to take root). Your asparagus will be ready in about 1 week, depending on the season and kitchen temperature and how tangy you like it. Cover and place in the refrigerator, where it will keep for about 3 months.

MEXICAN CHARRED CORN
WITH GREEK YOGURT AND SALTED PLUM VINEGAR

FEATURED FERMENTS: **GREEK YOGURT, UMEBOSHI VINEGAR**

———

Serves 4

Known as *esquites* in Spanish, this Mexican street food snack is an off-the-cob version of *elote*, the charred whole corn slathered with lime juice, chile powder, and mayonnaise you'll find all over Mexico. While some recipes call for removing the kernels and browning them in a cast-iron skillet, I like to roast them directly on my gas stovetop for a deliciously direct char (see Note). The dish is traditionally made with mayonnaise; I've switched it up by using Greek yogurt and heightened the sourness of the lime by including some umeboshi (salted plum) vinegar as well. It's great as an afternoon snack or a starter to a Mexican-themed main such as the pork stew on page 161.

4 ears corn, husked and silks removed

2 tablespoons Greek yogurt, homemade (page 37) or store-bought, plus more for serving

1 jalapeño chile, thinly sliced, seeds removed if you like (optional)

1 garlic clove, pressed through a garlic press

1½ tablespoons umeboshi vinegar, or to taste

1 tablespoon fresh lime juice, or to taste

¼ teaspoon ground cayenne, or to taste, plus more for an optional garnish

Small handful of fresh cilantro leaves, chopped

Small handful of fresh mint leaves, chopped

Turn four of your stove's gas burners to medium. Place the corn directly over the burners and cook, turning with tongs or the corn's handle every minute or so, until slightly softened and blackened, about 10 minutes. Do not leave the stove at any time while you are tending to your corn.

Cool slightly, then place a corn cob in a shallow bowl and using a paring knife, cut the kernels from the cob (keeping the operation contained in a bowl avoids stray kernels escaping). Repeat with the remaining corn cobs. Add the yogurt, jalapeño, garlic, vinegar, lime juice, cayenne, cilantro, and mint and stir to combine. Divide among bowls and serve warm, topping each bowl with a dollop of yogurt and a sprinkling of cayenne if you like. Alternatively, set aside for 30 minutes or so to let the flavors blend and intensify and serve at room temperature or refrigerate and serve cold.

NOTE: If you have an electric stove, you will need to use the skillet method: Heat a cast-iron grill pan or skillet over medium-high heat until good and hot, about 5 minutes. Add the corn cobs (you may have to break off the corn's handle to fit it level in the pan) and grill for about 15 minutes, turning every few minutes with tongs, until blackened all over.

SWAPS: Use Cultured Mayonnaise (page 82), Kefir Cream Cheese (page 40), or Countertop Crème Fraîche (page 79) instead of the Greek yogurt, or for a vegan option, try cultured Coconut Kefir Cream (page 165).

HOT AND SWEET WINGS
WITH CREAMY GORGONZOLA DRESSING

FEATURED FERMENTS: **KIMCHI JUICE, FISH SAUCE,
LIVE AND KICKIN' HOT SAUCE, CREAMY GORGONZOLA DRESSING**
SUPPORTING FERMENT: **SHRIMP PASTE**

———

Serves 4 as a starter or 2 as a meal

On a recent Sunday, generally my day off from the kitchen, my husband, Nash, set out to make a tried-and-true weekend dinner standby, oven-roasted chicken wings. With my kitchen the hotbed of fermentation that it is, it came as no surprise that four ferments—kimchi juice, fish sauce, hot sauce, and shrimp paste—made it into the marinade that day. A fifth and final fermentation flourish was a creamy kefir-based dressing to dip our juiced-up wings in.

While I've included this recipe in the starters and sides section, at my house we generally split a batch, serve with some potatoes that we've roasted while the oven's on, throw in some greens, and make a meal of it.

2 pounds (900 grams) pastured chicken wings, cut in half, tips trimmed and saved for stock

2 tablespoons Live and Kickin' Hot Sauce (page 81), or to taste

1 tablespoon kimchi juice (page 25) or brine from another pickled vegetable

1 tablespoon fish sauce

1/2 teaspoon shrimp paste (optional; see Note)

1/2 teaspoon fine sea salt

2 tablespoons maple syrup

1 lime, cut into wedges

Creamy gorgonzola dressing (see Tip, page 90)

Preheat the oven to 425°F (220°C) and line a baking sheet with a silicone liner or a sheet of parchment paper.

Put the wings in a large bowl. In a small bowl, combine the hot sauce, kimchi juice, fish sauce, shrimp paste, if using, and salt and whisk to dissolve the shrimp paste. Pour the marinade over the wings and stir well to coat, or put on disposable gloves and massage the marinade in. You can make the recipe to this point up to a day ahead; cover and keep refrigerated until you're ready to roast.

Transfer the wings to the baking sheet with a little space between each and roast for about 30 minutes, flipping them once, until nicely browned on both sides. Remove the wings from the oven, brush them with the maple syrup, return to the oven, and roast for another 5 minutes, or until a nice glaze covers the wings. Serve immediately, with lime wedges alongside and the dressing for dipping.

NOTE: If you double the recipe (as I often do), keep the pungent shrimp paste at 1/2 teaspoon.

SHORTCUT SALT-CURED SALMON PLATTERS

Serves 4

This recipe is based on Jacques Pépin's Instant Gravlax, which uses a technique that shortens curing time for salmon from days to just thirty minutes. The salmon is thinly sliced, salted, and stacked on plates; the salt melts into the salmon to shortcut cure it into gravlax. Pungent turnips and delicate but intensely lemony preserved lemon take this salad into tart and tangy new territory.

You'll need a freshly sharpened knife to slice the salmon into thin, even slices. Favor wild salmon over farmed for this recipe, as the difference in taste as well as environmental impact is huge. Watch your labels, especially folks on the East Coast; my friend the environmental writer Mary Thill recently enlightened me to the fact that contrary to the images of salmon swimming happily across the Atlantic ocean, fish with the label ATLANTIC SALMON are in most cases farmed salmon.

1½ teaspoons coarse sea salt

½ teaspoon coarsely ground black pepper, plus more for serving

12 ounces (340 grams) wild salmon fillet, bones removed

1 baby turnip, fresh or fermented (page 120), cut into matchsticks

2 teaspoons finely chopped Preserved Lemon peel (page 100) or drained and rinsed capers

Extra-virgin olive oil

4 handfuls of sunflower sprouts or microgreens

4 lemon wedges

In a small bowl, combine the salt and pepper.

Slice the salmon as thinly as possible at a slight angle across the length of the fillet using a zigzag motion, stopping at the fatty part attached to the skin.

Set out four large serving plates and sprinkle them evenly with half of the salt and pepper mixture. Divide the salmon among the plates, laying the slices flat on

top of the salt and pepper; do not overlap the slices. Sprinkle the salmon with the remaining salt and pepper mixture. Cover the plates with plastic wrap, pressing on the wrap so it sticks to the salmon and forms an airtight seal. Stack the plates one on top of the other to give them some weight and place an extra empty plate on top of the last plate to weight it, too. Refrigerate for at least 30 minutes or up to 24 hours.

Uncover the plates and sprinkle the turnips and preserved lemon over the salmon. Generously drizzle with oil, coarsely grind some black pepper over the plates, and place a handful of sprouts in the middle of each plate. Serve with the lemon wedges alongside.

SHORTCUT: Purchase prepared gravlax in a package from the fish counter; make sure the package indicates that it is cold smoked rather than hot smoked to ensure that the salmon is only cured and not cooked. The brand Spence & Co. is a good choice.

CHAPTER SIX

MAIN DISHES

TEMPEH IN COCONUT CHILE-BEAN SAUCE

FEATURED FERMENT: **TEMPEH**
SUPPORTING FERMENTS:
APPLE CIDER VINEGAR, CHILE-BEAN SAUCE, TAMARI

Serves 2 to 3

Tempeh hails from Indonesia, where it's a traditional source of protein; in this recipe it's cooked in coconut milk and Asian seasonings designed to hit a variety of notes: spicy from the chile-bean sauce, salty from the tamari, tangy from the vinegar and lime juice, and sweet from the maple syrup.

I think of tempeh as a healthy fast-food ferment, as I've never been DIY enough to incubate my own soybeans to turn them into fermented soy cakes. I look for good-quality brands made with organic soybeans (most nonorganic soy is genetically modified), and all I have to do is open a package to get my tempeh fix. (If you'd like to learn how to make your own, take a look at 1970s fermentation pioneer William Shurtleff's classic *Book of Tempeh: A Super Soyfood from Indonesia*.) This dish uses all store-bought ferments, perfect for those of us who want our culture but also the convenience of a meal in less than thirty minutes. Atop rice or another grain of your choice, this makes an easy complete meal.

1/4 cup (60 milliliters) unrefined virgin coconut oil, plus more if needed

1 (8-ounce/227-gram) package tempeh, cut into 1/2-inch (12 millimeter) squares

1 large red onion, cut into thick slices

1 (2-inch/5-centimeter) piece fresh ginger, minced

2 garlic cloves, chopped

1 tablespoon raw apple cider vinegar

1/2 cup (120 milliliters) Vegetable Broth (page 109), Traditional Broth (page 108), or water

3/4 cup (180 milliliters) coconut milk

2 tablespoons fermented chile-bean sauce (available at Asian food stores)

2 tablespoons maple syrup, plus more if needed

1 teaspoon tamari

1/2 teaspoon fine sea salt, plus more if needed

2 bunches baby bok choy or other Asian green such as choy sum or tatsoi, chopped

1 tablespoon fresh lime juice, plus more if needed

Heat the coconut oil in a medium sauté pan over medium-high heat. Add the tempeh and cook for about 3 minutes, until browned on the bottom. Flip the pieces with tongs and cook for another 3 minutes or so, until browned on the second side. Transfer to a plate. Add the onion to the pan, adding more oil if the pan has gone dry, and cook, stirring often, for 5 minutes, or until well browned. Add the ginger and cook for 2 minutes; add the garlic and cook for another 2 minutes, or until softened and everything is deeply browned. Add the vinegar and stir to release any browned bits from the bottom of the pan.

Add the broth, 1/2 cup (120 milliliters) of the coconut milk, the chile-bean sauce, maple syrup, tamari, and salt. Bring to a simmer, then add the tempeh. Return to a simmer, then reduce the heat to low, cover, and simmer for about 20 minutes. If the sauce is still too thin, uncover the pan, raise the heat, and cook for a few minutes to thicken it. Stir in the bok choy and cook for about 2 minutes, until softened but still crisp. Stir in the remaining 1/4 cup (60 milliliters) coconut milk and cook just to heat through. Add the lime juice. Taste and adjust the seasonings with salt, lime juice, and/or maple syrup. Serve immediately over rice or another grain of your choice.

FETTUCCINE-STYLE ZUCCHINI

FEATURED FERMENT: CULTURED SAUCE SUCH AS CILANTRO-MISO PESTO, SWEET LEMON MISO TAHINI DRESSING, OR GIARDINIERA

Serves 1 or more

Noodles made from zucchini are a popular new pasta choice, as they satisfy both raw foodists and those looking for gluten-free and low-carb alternatives to standard wheat pasta. The blank-canvas quality of zucchini makes it an ideal base for showcasing any number of sauces; use one of the options I've given here or any of your favorite ferment-based toppings.

Zucchini noodles are easy to make, but do require a small investment in a spiral slicer or Swiss vegetable peeler, which you can find at many kitchen stores and online. One medium zucchini generally serves one person, so if you're going solo for dinner, spiralize a single zucchini and toss with as much sauce as needed.

1 medium zucchini per person, ends trimmed

Cultured sauce of your choice, such as cilantro-miso pesto (see page 136) thinned with a little oil or water, sweet lemon miso tahini dressing (see page 92), or juice from Giardiniera (see page 123)

Extra-virgin olive oil

Fresh lemon juice, pickle juice (page 29), or another acid flavoring as needed

Miso Parmesan (optional; page 85)

Cut the zucchini into fettuccine shapes (or alternatively, spaghetti noodle shapes) with a spiralizer or shave with a Swiss vegetable peeler. Put the zucchini noodles in a bowl, and leave for 30 minutes to release a little of their moisture. Pat and squeeze the moisture from the zucchini with paper towels. Toss the zucchini with sauce to coat. Taste and adjust the consistency and seasonings, adding olive oil and lemon juice, pickle juice, or another acid if some brightness is needed to round out the dish. Serve topped with Miso Parmesan, if you like.

SWAP: Toss with any of the cultured salad dressings on pages 88 and 89.

COLLARD GREEN WRAP
WITH CREAMY CASHEW CHEESE AND SWEET MANGO CHUTNEY

FEATURED FERMENTS: **CREAMY CASHEW CHEESE, SWEET MANGO CHUTNEY**
SUPPORTING FERMENT: **PICKLED CARROTS**

Makes 4 wraps

A collard green leaf makes a handy wrapper to spread with any number of fillings, such as this duo of flavorful ferments. It's light, gluten free, and a creative way of enjoying your greens, though of course the cheese and chutney can be spread over your choice of bread, traditional sandwich style.

4 large collard green leaves

1 cup (240 grams) Creamy Cashew Cheese (page 83)

About 8 tablespoons Sweet Mango Chutney (page 78)

4 tablespoons chopped fresh mint or cilantro leaves

1/2 cup pickled grated carrots (page 32), or 2 fresh carrots, coarsely grated

4 handfuls of sunflower or other sprouts or arugula leaves

Place a collard leaf on a cutting board and, using a sharp knife, trim off the thick part of the stem. Spread 1/4 cup (60 grams) of the cashew cheese over the leaf, leaving 1/2 inch (12 millimeters) space on the sides. Spread about 2 tablespoons of the chutney over the cheese (if your chutney is liquidy, scoop it out with a slotted spoon), then sprinkle one quarter each of the mint, carrots, and sprouts on top.

Working from the end facing you, tightly roll the collard leaf away from you, tucking in the ends after the roll is completed if you like. Place seam side down and cut the wrap in half using a serrated knife. Place on a plate; repeat with the remaining collard leaves and filling. Serve immediately.

SWAP: Use All-Around Almond Cheese (page 84) in place of the cashew cheese.

MILLET POLENTA CAKES WITH ZUCCHINI, DAIKON, CHERRY TOMATOES, AND CILANTRO-MISO PESTO

FEATURED FERMENT: **FERMENTED MILLET**
SUPPORTING FERMENTS: **MISO, GREEK YOGURT**

———————

Serves 3 to 4

This recipe is an extension of the millet porridge concept on page 48 (and a riff on the French-style chickpea flour–based bites known as *panisse*); after you've made your porridge, you pour it onto a baking sheet to firm up, then cut it into squares or circles and bake to crisp it (it firms up very quickly, so be prepared to pour just as it comes off the burner).

Millet polenta is open to endless variations, serving as the base for any number of meat or vegetable toppings; the one I've presented here features a light and flavorful medley of summer vegetables and a miso-based pesto for a little extra culture and dairy-free flavor. To make this dish completely dairy free, pass on the yogurt topping. You can cook the polenta a day ahead of time; pour it into the baking sheet, cool, and refrigerate until you're ready to bake it.

Millet polenta freezes well (freeze it before baking), so feel free to double up the base polenta recipe and keep some on hand to heat up as you like. Or take your double recipe and make meals with it through the week: I like it for breakfast with a fried egg and hot sauce, and I'll warm up a square to serve as the carb portion of my lunch or dinner. A toasted polenta square drizzled with maple syrup makes a sweet midday treat.

MILLET POLENTA

Extra-virgin olive oil, for the pan and brushing

1 recipe just-cooked Savory Millet Porridge (page 48)

PESTO

1 to 2 garlic cloves, peeled

1 bunch fresh cilantro, leaves and stems, chopped

1 cup (120 grams) pine nuts or hulled pumpkin seeds or a mixture

2 to 3 tablespoons light miso

3 tablespoons fresh lime juice, or to taste

1/4 teaspoon freshly ground black pepper

Fine sea salt, if needed

1/2 cup (120 milliliters) extra-virgin olive oil

VEGETABLES

2 tablespoons extra-virgin olive oil

1 garlic clove, minced

1 pound (450 grams/2 to 3) zucchini, chopped

1 small daikon root, chopped

1 cup (125 grams) cherry tomatoes, quartered

1 scallion, white and green parts, finely chopped

1 tablespoon fresh lemon juice, or to taste

1/2 teaspoon fine sea salt, or to taste

TO SERVE

Greek yogurt, homemade (page 37) or store-bought (optional)

Freshly ground black pepper

Make the millet polenta: Preheat the oven to 375°F (190°C). Grease a 9-inch (23-centimeter) square baking dish and a baking sheet.

As the millet porridge is cooked, immediately pour it from the pan into the prepared baking dish. Spread the mixture out evenly with a spatula and set aside to cool and set for about 1 hour.

When the polenta is set, cut it into 9 equal squares. (Alternatively, you could use a round or other shape cookie cutter to form various-shaped cakes.) Place the squares on the greased baking sheet, brush with oil, and bake until the edges start to brown but the inside remains soft, 30 to 35 minutes. While the millet is in the oven, make the pesto and vegetables.

Make the pesto: With the motor of a food processor running, drop the garlic in through the feed tube to mince it. Add the remaining ingredients except the salt and oil and process to combine. With the motor running, drizzle in the oil through the hole in the lid and process until smooth. Taste and add salt and/or more lime juice if needed. You could make the pesto a day or two in advance.

Make the vegetables: Heat the oil in a large saucepan over medium heat. Add the garlic and cook for about 1 minute, until just starting to color. Add the zucchini and daikon and cook for about 5 minutes, until softened but still al dente. Add the tomatoes and cook for about 2 minutes, until softened. Remove from the heat and stir in the scallion. Add the lemon juice and salt; taste and add more lemon juice and/or salt if needed.

Arrange 2 or 3 polenta squares on each serving plate. Top with the vegetables and drizzle with pesto. Finish with a dollop of yogurt and a few grinds of the peppermill.

TEFF FLATBREAD
WITH ETHIOPIAN-STYLE SPICY RED LENTILS

FEATURED FERMENT: **FERMENTED TEFF**

———

Serves 4 to 6, with leftover batter (makes about 6 cups/1.5 liters batter)

This flatbread, based on Ethiopian *injera*, is made from tiny teff, the world's smallest grain. Injera is a national dish of Ethiopia and eaten at just about every meal in that country, with food served atop the bread and more rolled up alongside for scooping. The word *teff* means "lost" in Amharic because, according to the story, grains that fall on the ground are so small they become lost. Teff has an earthy, slightly bitter taste, and when fermented it has an assertive, deliciously sour flavor. Sometimes injera is cut with wheat flour to trim costs and lighten it up (as well as add to the spongy texture you'll find in restaurant versions; mine has a little crispness to it), but I make this flatbread 100 percent teff to keep it gluten free, intensely dark, and deeply nourishing. Here the flatbread is served with a spicy lentil stew but would work equally well with any stew-type meat, bean, or vegetable dish that lends itself to scooping.

4 cups (680 grams) teff flour (see Note)

5 cups (1.2 liters) filtered water (see Note, page 61)

1½ teaspoons fine sea salt

1 teaspoon baking powder

Unrefined virgin coconut oil

Ethiopian Spicy Red Lentils (recipe follows on page 140)

Steamed kale or other greens

Put the teff flour in a large bowl. Whisk in the water until a smooth batter is formed. Cover the bowl with a plate or clean dish towel and let sit for 36 to 48 hours, depending on the season and kitchen temperature, until the batter is foamy, risen, and smells slightly sour and earthy.

Heat a very well seasoned 10- or 12-inch (25- or 30-centimeter) cast-iron or nonstick skillet over medium-high heat. Whisk the batter to deflate it, then whisk the salt into the batter, and, finally, whisk in the baking powder. The consistency should be that of thin pancake batter (if it's not, add a little water).

Very lightly coat the bottom of the skillet with coconut oil. Ladle in ⅓ to ½ cup (80 to 120 milliliters) of the batter (depending on the size of the skillet); tilt the skillet and swirl the batter so it covers the bottom of the skillet. Cook until holes form all over the surface, about 1 minute, then cover the skillet and steam for about 2 minutes, until the flatbread is cooked through and slightly glossy on the surface and the edges pull away from the sides of the pan (don't flip it, as it cooks on one side only). Use a spatula to remove the flatbread from the skillet to a plate and repeat making flatbread (the flatbread can be served warm or at room temperature). Serve, with the lentils and kale alongside.

NOTE: Teff flour can be found in some natural food stores or online (see Resources, page 183). For the freshest flour, buy whole teff and grind it in a spice mill. Leftover batter will keep, refrigerated, for about a week.

ETHIOPIAN-STYLE SPICY RED LENTILS

Serves 6

Known as *misir wot* in the cuisine of Ethiopia, this hearty lentil stew is flavored by berbere, a complex assortment of spices reflecting the diverse cultural influences on Ethiopia. If you're not up for making your own, you can find the blend in international groceries or online (see Resources, page 183).

BERBERE SPICE BLEND
(MAKES ABOUT 1/2 CUP/60 GRAMS)

5 dried red árbol or other small chiles

2 teaspoons cumin seeds

2 teaspoons cardamom pods

2 teaspoons coriander seeds

1 teaspoon fenugreek seeds

1/2 teaspoon whole black peppercorns

1/4 teaspoon whole cloves

3 tablespoons mild paprika

1 teaspoon ground ginger

1 teaspoon ground turmeric

1/2 teaspoon ground allspice

1/2 teaspoon ground cinnamon

1 teaspoon fine sea salt

LENTILS

1 1/2 cups (300 grams) dried red lentils

2 tablespoons raw apple cider vinegar

3 tablespoons cultured butter (see page 53), unrefined virgin coconut oil, or extra-virgin olive oil

1 large onion, finely chopped

2 tablespoons ginger-garlic paste (see page 155)

2 tablespoons tomato paste

1/2 teaspoon fine sea salt, or to taste

Fresh lemon juice

Countertop Crème Fraîche (page 79; optional)

Make the berbere spice blend: Heat a small cast-iron skillet over medium heat until hot. Add the chiles and toast for about 15 seconds on each side, until browned. Transfer to a plate. Add the cumin seeds, cardamom pods, coriander seeds, fenugreek seeds, peppercorns, and cloves to the pan and toast, stirring continously, for 2 to 3 minutes, until fragrant and lightly browned. Transfer to the plate with the chiles and let cool. Remove the stems from the chiles and some or all of the seeds if you'd like to tame the heat. Break up the chiles, put the chiles and toasted whole spices in a spice grinder, and grind until finely ground. Let the spices settle with the cover remaining on the spice grinder for about a minute. Transfer the mixture to a bowl and add the paprika, ginger, turmeric, allspice, cinnamon, and salt. Stir to blend the spices. Transfer to an airtight container and store for up to 6 months.

Make the lentils: Rinse the lentils in a glass bowl or measuring cup until the water runs clear, then drain. Put the lentils in a bowl and add the vinegar and 4 cups (1 liter) water. Cover with a plate or clean dish towel and set aside for about 24 hours. (See page 49 to learn why it's important to soak grains and beans.) Drain and rinse the lentils again.

Heat 2 tablespoons of the butter in a large saucepan over medium heat. Add the onion and sauté for about 5 minutes, until softened. Add the ginger-garlic paste and sauté for another 2 minutes. Add 1 to 3 tablespoons of the berbere spice blend, to taste, and cook, stirring, for about 2 minutes, until aromatic, adding a little water to the pan if it starts getting dry. Add 3 cups (720 milliliters) water, stirring to release any browned bits stuck to the bottom of the pan, then add the tomato paste and lentils. Bring to a simmer, cover, reduce the heat to low, and simmer until the lentils are very tender and falling apart and the stew is a consistency in between porridge and soup, about 45 minutes, adding more water if needed. Stir in the remaining 1 tablespoon butter and add the salt and lemon juice to taste. Serve with teff flatbread, topped with some crème fraîche if you like.

GREEK-STYLE TURKEY MEATBALLS
WITH TZATZIKI SAUCE

FEATURED FERMENT: **YOGURT**

———

Serves 4

The cucumber and yogurt sauce known as tzatziki is usually used as a dip or spread; here I've made it into a sauce that's tossed with just-out-of-the-oven Greek-spice turkey meatballs that warm the yogurt, but not too much, so it maintains its active culture content, and is served over rice or another grain.

MEATBALLS

Extra-virgin olive oil, for baking and finishing

1½ pounds (680 grams) pastured ground turkey, preferably dark meat

1/3 cup (50 grams) finely chopped red onion

1/4 cup (60 milliliters) Greek yogurt, homemade (page 37) or store-bought

8 sun-dried tomato halves, soaked in hot water to cover for 2 hours, then drained and minced (optional)

2 garlic cloves, pressed through a garlic press

2 tablespoons minced fresh dill, or 2 teaspoons dried dill

2 tablespoons minced fresh flat-leaf parsley

2 teaspoons finely grated lemon zest

1½ teaspoons fine sea salt

1/4 to 1/2 teaspoon ground cayenne

TZATZIKI SAUCE

3 cups (720 milliliters) yogurt, homemade (page 34) or store-bought

1/2 cup (60 grams) minced peeled and seeded cucumber (about 1/2 cucumber)

2 tablespoons fresh lemon juice, or to taste

1/2 cup (30 grams) chopped fresh mint

1 teaspoon fine sea salt, or to taste

1/4 teaspoon freshly ground black pepper, or to taste

FOR SERVING

Hot rice

Extra-virgin olive oil

1 cup (125 grams) cherry tomatoes, cut in half

1/4 cup (30 grams) pine nuts, toasted

Chopped fresh mint

Make the meatballs: Preheat the oven to 400°F (200°C). Line a rimmed baking sheet with parchment paper or aluminum foil and oil the parchment.

In a large bowl, combine all the ingredients; wearing a disposable glove or using your just-washed hands, mix very well (the yogurt will make the meat very soft, which is fine). Form the mixture into about 24 equal-size balls measuring about 1½ inches (4 centimeters) each. Place the meatballs on the prepared baking sheet and brush with a little more oil. Bake for about 25 minutes, until the meatballs are browned and when you cut into a sample meatball you see that the meat inside is no longer pink.

Make the tzatziki sauce: Put the yogurt in a large serving bowl and whisk it to give it a smooth consistency. Stir in the remaining ingredients; taste and adjust the seasonings.

As soon as the meatballs come out of the oven, stir them into the yogurt sauce. Taste and adjust the seasonings. Spoon into bowls over hot rice. Finish with a drizzle of oil, a generous grinding of pepper, and some cherry tomatoes, pine nuts, and mint.

FISH TACOS WITH THE WORKS

FEATURED FERMENT OPTIONS: **LIVE AND KICKIN' HOT SAUCE; SALSA ALIVE OR SMOKY PEACH, CHERRY TOMATO, AND BASIL SALSA; SALSA VERDE; GUACAMOLE WITH A KICK; SAUERKRAUT OR KIMCHI; PICKLE SALAD; GIARDINIERA; COUNTERTOP CRÈME FRAÎCHE**

Makes 8 tacos

These tacos are loaded, perfect for a party and a platform for your finest ferments. Pile 'em on.

16 corn tortillas, such as Ezekiel brand sprouted corn tortillas

1½ pounds (680 grams) skinless wild-caught firm white fish fillet, such as cod or catfish, sliced ¼ inch (6 milliliters) thick

1 teaspoon fine sea salt

1½ teaspoons ancho chile powder or sweet paprika

1 tablespoon extra-virgin olive oil

¼ cup (60 milliliters) fresh lime juice

Handful of chopped fresh cilantro

TOPPING OPTIONS

Live and Kickin' Hot Sauce (page 81)

Salsa Alive (page 76) or Smoky Peach, Cherry Tomato, and Basil Salsa (page 78)

Salsa Verde (page 75)

Guacamole with a Kick (page 116)

Sauerkraut (page 23) or Kimchi (page 25)

Pickle Salad (page 101)

Giardiniera (page 123)

Countertop Crème Fraîche (page 79)

Prepare a steamer by filling it with 2 inches (5 centimeters) of water and bringing it to a boil over medium-high heat. Wrap the tortillas in a kitchen towel, place them in the steamer insert, and cover the steamer. Reduce the heat to a simmer and steam the tortillas for 2 minutes. Turn off the heat and let them stand, covered, for up to 30 minutes while you prepare the fish.

In a large bowl, combine the fish, salt, and chile powder. With clean hands or wearing disposable kitchen gloves, massage the spices into the fish for a couple of minutes to thoroughly season the fish.

Heat the oil in a large sauté, pan over medium-high heat. Add the fish and sauté, tossing frequently, until just cooked through, 3 to 4 minutes. Remove from the heat and stir in the lime juice. Transfer the fish to a serving bowl and stir in the cilantro.

To serve, grab two tortillas for each taco (when doubled up they keep the filling in more securely). Top with some fish using a slotted spoon, and pile on any of the suggested toppings.

GALETTES

———

Makes about 10 crêpes

A galette is a thin buckwheat-based savory crêpe hailing from the Brittany region of France. Here I've fermented the buckwheat to add a sourdough flavor that complements the earthiness of the grain. (See page 49 for more on how our ancestors fermented their grains.) How you fill your galette is up to you. You can go traditional with a ham, egg, and cheese combo; try out one of my other suggestions; or come up with a filling of your own.

1 cup (140 grams) untoasted buckwheat groats (not kasha, which is toasted and a shade darker)

2 tablespoons raw apple cider vinegar or other starter culture (see page 20)

2 large farm-fresh eggs

1/2 teaspoon fine sea salt

Unrefined virgin coconut oil or cultured butter (see page 53)

FILLING OPTIONS

Ham and fried egg with shredded Gruyère or Emmenthal cheese

Caramelized leeks and fried egg, with or without the cheese

Fried tempeh cubes, sauerkraut, and Juiced-up Mustard (page 73)

Guacamole with a Kick (page 116), feta cheese, and sliced cucumber

Pulled pork and Sweet Mango Chutney (page 78)

Ethiopian-Style Spicy Red Lentils (page 140) and Countertop Crème Fraîche (page 79)

Chicken Masala (page 154)

Put the buckwheat in a large bowl. Add the vinegar and 3 cups (720 milliliters) water. Cover with a clean dish towel and leave to ferment for 12 to 24 hours, depending on the season and kitchen temperature.

It will look a little cloudy and smell slightly fermented, but it won't change much. Drain and rinse well. The buckwheat will be sticky; try to rinse most of the stickiness off, but it's okay if you don't get it all. Transfer the buckwheat to a blender, add 1 cup (240 milliliters) water, and blend until smooth. Transfer to a clean bowl, cover, and set aside to ferment again for 12 to 24 hours, until there is a slight sourdough smell.

Heat a large well-seasoned cast-iron or nonstick skillet over medium heat until hot, 3 to 5 minutes. While it's heating up, whisk the eggs and salt into the buckwheat. Add more water if the batter is too thick.

Add a very small amount of oil to the pan and brush or wipe it around with a paper towel to coat the skillet evenly. Using a bowl or measuring cup with a spout, pour in about 1/4 cup (60 milliliters) batter, just enough to coat the pan, quickly tilting so the batter spreads across the entire pan in a thin layer. Cook until the crêpe sets and the sides start to curl, about 1 minute. Run a nonstick spatula under the crêpe, flip it, and cook for another 30 seconds or so, until the second side is firm. Remove from the skillet and repeat with the remaining batter. To keep your crêpes warm until serving time, fold them in half, place in a baking pan, cover with foil, and place in a preheated 200°F (95°C) oven as they come off the skillet. Add your chosen filling to the crêpes just before serving.

THE CULTURED BURGER

FEATURED FERMENT OPTIONS:
JUICED-UP MUSTARD, WAKE-UP KETCHUP, CULTURED MAYONNAISE, THICK GORGONZOLA KEFIR DRESSING, ASIAN-STYLE PICKLE SALAD, GIARDINIERA

Serves 4

This burger is a showcase for the very best beef available to you and any combination of your favorite ferments. Mix and match for a signature cultured burger; serve it on a bun or naked over a bed of sautéed kale if you like.

1½ pounds (680 grams) pastured ground beef chuck

1 teaspoon fine salt

½ teaspoon freshly ground black pepper

Buns or a bed of sautéed kale (optional)

CULTURED CONDIMENTS

Juiced-up Mustard (page 73)

Wake-up Ketchup (page 74)

Cultured Mayonnaise (page 82)

Thick Gorgonzola Kefir Dressing (see Tip, page 90)

Asian-Style Pickle Salad (page 101)

Giardiniera (page 123)

Combine the beef and salt in a large bowl and mix gently but thoroughly. Divide the mixture into four equal portions and form each into a loose ball. Pat tightly to flatten the meat into a burger ¾ inch (2 centimeters) thick. Press the center of the patties down with your fingertips until about ½ inch (12 millimeters) thick to create an indentation in the center, resulting in edges that are thicker than the center (a tip for keeping your burgers from puffing up as they cook).

Heat a large heavy-bottomed skillet, preferably cast-iron, over medium-high heat until very hot. Add the patties, indentation side up, and cook on each side for about 3 minutes for rare, 3½ minutes for medium-rare, 4 minutes for medium, and 5 minutes for well-done. Serve immediately, in buns or over kale if you like, garnished with your choice of condiments.

KOREAN-STYLE RICE BOWL WITH KIMCHI

FEATURED FERMENT: **KIMCHI**
SUPPORTING FERMENTS: **TAMARI, LIVE AND KICKIN' HOT SAUCE**

———

Serves 2 or 3

This takes a standard Korean rice dish, kimchi *bokkeumbap*, and brings new life to it by adding the kimchi after cooking instead of frying it at the beginning. It's also a great way of using leftover rice and making a healthy dent in the kimchi jar. To make your rice bowl vegetarian, make the kimchi without fish sauce or shrimp paste, pass on the shredded meat option, and omit the bacon.

1 tablespoon unrefined plain sesame oil or cultured butter (see page 53)

1 onion, chopped

2 garlic cloves, chopped

1 tablespoon tamari

3 cups (360 grams) cold or room-temperature (not hot) cooked rice

Couple of handfuls of shredded cooked leftover pastured chicken, beef, or pork, or cubed, drained, and patted-dry firm tofu (optional)

1 teaspoon toasted sesame oil

1 cup (260 grams) drained and chopped kimchi, homemade (page 25) or store-bought, at room temperature

Kimchi juice (page 25)

Live and Kickin' Hot Sauce (page 81), Korean red pepper paste, or Sriracha sauce

4 slices cooked farmhouse bacon (optional; see recipe on page 52 for tips on cooking bacon), crumbled

Topping options: fried farm-fresh eggs, sliced scallions or chopped fresh cilantro, slivers of nori seaweed (cut with scissors), toasted sesame seeds

Heat the plain sesame oil in a large skillet over medium heat. Add the onion and sauté for about 5 minutes, until softened. Add the garlic and cook for 1 minute. Add the tamari and cook for 2 minutes. Add the rice and meat or tofu, if using, and heat until hot. Remove from the heat and stir in the toasted sesame oil and kimchi. Taste and add kimchi juice and hot sauce until you've got it just right for your taste. Serve immediately, sprinkled with bacon, if you like, and with your choice of additional toppings.

SHRIMP PAD THAI WITH PRESERVED RADISH

FEATURED FERMENT: **PRESERVED RADISH**
SUPPORTING FERMENTS: **FISH SAUCE, SHRIMP PASTE**

———

Serves 2 or 3

This pad Thai may taste somewhat different from the one you've had at the Thai restaurant down the block. The difference is in the preserved radish, an ingredient that gets left out of many restaurant pad Thais and that when included provides a subtle salty-sweet crunch and authenticity to the dish. An ample amount of fish sauce and shrimp paste add to that real Thai feeling. These three ingredients are available at Asian food stores. In this dish our ferments are cooked, making use of their elevated flavoring profile. They are here for the pure pleasure they provide!

¼ cup (60 milliliters) fish sauce

¼ cup (50 grams) packed palm sugar or other unrefined brown sugar

2 teaspoons shrimp paste

½ teaspoon tamarind concentrate

4 tablespoons unrefined sesame oil

7 ounces (200 grams) medium-thin rice noodles (⅛ inch/3 millimeters thick), soaked in warm water to cover for about 30 minutes, until pliable but still firm, then drained

2 large garlic cloves, minced

1 shallot, minced

⅓ cup (35 grams) finely chopped preserved radish

8 ounces (225 grams) large fresh shrimp, peeled and deveined

2 large farm-fresh eggs, cracked into a bowl

4 scallions, white and green parts, sliced

1½ cups (150 grams) bean sprouts

Garnishes: more fish sauce, lime wedges, red chile flakes, chopped roasted peanuts, more bean sprouts, and more scallion slices

In small saucepan, combine the fish sauce, palm sugar, shrimp paste, and tamarind. Place over medium heat and stir until the sugar dissolves, about 1 minute.

Heat a very large skillet (14 inches/36 centimeters wide, if available), over medium-high heat. Add 2 tablespoons of the sesame oil. Let the oil heat up for a couple of seconds, then add the noodles and stir using tongs to coat them with the oil. Add the fish sauce mixture. Cook, stirring continously with the tongs, for about 1 minute, until the noodles have softened but are still al dente and the sauce has been absorbed.

Push the noodles to one side of the pan and add the remaining 2 tablespoons sesame oil to the empty side. Add the garlic, shallot, and preserved radish to the top side of the empty part of the pan and the fresh shrimp to the bottom side. Cook, stirring the garlic and shallots and turning the shrimp once, until the shrimp just turns pink and the garlic and shallots start to brown, about 3 minutes. (Continue to stir the noodles on the other side.) Stir the shrimp mixture into the noodles.

Make a well in the middle of the pan and add the eggs. Beat the eggs and cook without moving them until just set on the underside, about 2 minutes, then break into smaller pieces. The shrimp should be fully cooked, the noodles softened, and the sauce absorbed; if not, cook for another minute or two. Give it a final stir.

Remove from the heat and stir in the scallions and bean sprouts. Serve immediately, with your choice of garnishes.

CRUNCHY KIMCHI PORK

FEATURED FERMENT: **KIMCHI**
SUPPORTING FERMENTS: **FISH SAUCE, LIVE AND KICKIN' HOT SAUCE**

———

Serves 2 or 3

This hearty salad-as-a-meal is inspired by a Thai limey ground pork and herb salad called *larb*, one of my all-time favorite comfort foods. It's super-easy to put together: Just cook up the pork, add the kimchi and seasonings, and a powerfully flavorful dinner is on the table in less than twenty minutes.

The amount of seasoning you'll use depends on how salty, tangy, and spicy your current batch of kimchi is, so after you've mixed the pork and kimchi, taste and go from there, adding fish sauce or salt, vinegar, and hot sauce until you've reached your personal flavoring sweet spot. The toasted rice adds a pleasing little crunch, but it's optional if you don't have the time or a spice grinder on hand. In fact, you could get away with making this dish with just two ingredients: kimchi and pork; I like to have a pound of pork in the freezer and ample kimchi on hand at all times for just that purpose. Serve over rice or rice noodles, or set atop lettuce leaves for lighter fare.

1 pound (450 grams) ground pastured pork

1 tablespoon uncooked white rice (optional)

1½ cups (225 grams) kimchi, homemade (page 25) or store-bought, at room temperature

½ cup (20 grams) chopped fresh cilantro

Fish sauce or salt (optional)

Rice vinegar (optional)

Live and Kickin' Hot Sauce (page 81; optional)

Put the pork in a large skillet; heat over medium heat, stirring often, until cooked through, the fat releases, and the meat starts to brown and crisp, about 10 minutes.

Meanwhile, if you're using it, toast the rice in a small skillet over medium heat for 2 to 3 minutes, until very lightly browned and toasty smelling. Transfer to a spice grinder, cool for a couple of minutes, then grind to a coarse powder.

Transfer the pork to a large bowl and stir in the kimchi, ground rice, and cilantro. Taste and add fish sauce or salt, vinegar, and/or hot sauce to taste as needed depending on the potency of your batch of kimchi.

FROM TOP: Chicken Masala Dosa
(page 154) and Vegetarian Masala Dosa.

VEGETARIAN MASALA DOSA

Makes enough filling for 6 to 8 dosas

This is the standard dosa filling you'll find on South Indian restaurant menus, the Indian equivalent of mashed potatoes—comfort food with a kick! This version is the work of my husband, Nash Patel.

2 pounds (900 grams; about 8) boiling (waxy) potatoes

1/4 cup (60 milliliters) extra-virgin olive oil or unrefined virgin coconut oil

2 teaspoons black mustard seeds

2 teaspoons cumin seeds

16 curry leaves (see Note)

2 tablespoons chana dhal (optional; see Note), soaked in water to cover for 10 minutes and drained

1 large red onion, chopped

2 teaspoons minced fresh ginger

1 to 6 small green chiles, seeded if you like, minced

1/2 teaspoon ground turmeric

1/4 teaspoon ground cayenne

1/2 teaspoon fine sea salt, plus more if needed

Squeeze of lemon juice

South Indian Rice and Lentil Dosas (recipe follows on page 152)

Put the potatoes in a large saucepan, add water to cover, and place over medium-high heat. Bring to a boil, then reduce the heat and simmer for about 20 minutes, until the potatoes can be pierced easily with a knife. Drain, reserving about 1 cup (240 milliliters) of the cooking water. Cool the potatoes slightly, then remove the peels with your hands.

Return the potatoes to the pan and coarsely mash them with a potato masher.

In a small saucepan, heat the oil over medium-high heat. Add the mustard seeds and cumin seeds and cook for about 1 minute, until the spices are aromatic and the mustard seeds start to pop. Add the curry leaves and cook, stirring, for 30 seconds. Add the chana dhal, if using, stir, then add the onion and cook, stirring, for about 5 minutes, until well browned. Add the ginger and chiles and cook, stirring, for about 2 minutes, until softened. Add the turmeric, cayenne, and salt and cook for 30 seconds. Add 1/4 cup (60 milliliters) of the reserved potato cooking water and stir to release any browned bits from the bottom of the pan.

Add the onion mixture to the mashed potatoes and cook, stirring, for 10 minutes to blend the flavors, adding more potato cooking water if the mixture is too thick (it should be the consistency of roughly mashed potatoes). Add the lemon juice, taste, and season with additional salt if needed.

Serve, either rolled into your dosas or alongside, using the dosa as utensil.

NOTES: Aromatic curry leaves are a frequently used seasoning ingredient in South Indian cooking, and are no relation to the spice mix curry powder. Unlike bay leaves, they can be eaten after cooking. They can be found fresh or frozen in Indian groceries; skip dried curry leaves, as they have little flavor.

Chana dhal, made from chickpeas, is available at Indian groceries.

SOUTH INDIAN LENTIL AND RICE DOSAS

Makes about 2½ quarts (2.5 liters)
batter, for about 30 dosas

These are the sourdough-style crepes famous in South Indian cuisine, often served in a larger-than-life length of a couple of feet and extending off the plate they're presented on. Here we'll make them in a more doable-at-home 10-inch (25-centimeter) crêpe pan.

The batter makes enough for several meals of dosas; it keeps for a couple of months in the refrigerator (where it continues to sour slightly, varying the flavor of your dosas), so after all the work of soaking, blending, and fermenting, you'll have ample dosa batter in the fridge ready for cooking up dosas anytime the urge hits: Use them instead of rice with a curry or other dish or make them into sandwich wraps. My brother likes to use them as a gluten-free "bread" for his tuna fish sandwiches, and I fill them with scrambled eggs for breakfast. Drizzled with maple syrup, they make a Vermont-style dessert dosa.

Urad dhal, a split lentil, and fenugreek seeds are available at Indian groceries. One or two dosas per person is a general serving guideline.

1 cup (200 grams) split urad dhal

3 cups (570 grams) medium-grain white rice (not basmati)

1 teaspoon fenugreek seeds

2 teaspoons fine sea salt, plus more if needed

½ teaspoon baking soda

Unrefined sunflower oil

Put the urad dhal and rice in a large bowl and rinse with several changes of filtered water until the water is clear, then drain. Return the urad dhal and rice to the bowl and add the fenugreek seeds and 8 cups (2 liters) water. Cover with a dish towel and set aside in a warm place away from sunlight for about 8 hours or overnight.

Drain the urad dhal and rice. Transfer half of the mixture to a blender, add 1 cup (480 milliliters) water, and blend until smooth and the consistency of thick pancake batter, 2 to 3 minutes (a high-speed blender works particularly well for dosas, but a regular blender will do), adding a little more water if needed to thin it and keep the blender moving. Pour the blended mixture into a large bowl or container and repeat with the remaining urad dhal and rice, blending it with the same amount of water. Add the second batch to the first and stir.

Cover the bowl with a dish towel and keep it in a warm place for about 12 hours, more if your fermenting area is on the cool side. The ideal temperature for fermentation is 90°F (30°C), which is easily achieved in tropical southern India. If you have a dehydrator with removable shelves, you can set the temperature accordingly and ferment your dosa batter in it. (An alternative is placing the bowl on a heating pad set to the lowest temperature—make sure there is plenty of headroom in the bowl to minimize the chance of batter overflowing onto the heating pad.) The batter is done when it is thick and foamy, risen a bit, and has a light sour smell to it. Stir the batter, then stir in the salt, cover, and refrigerate it for at least 2 hours before making your dosas.

When you are ready to make your dosas, whisk the batter. It should be the consistency of pancake batter; if it isn't, add a little water. In a small bowl, dissolve the baking soda in 1 tablespoon water, then whisk it into the batter.

Heat a 10-inch (25-centimeter) crêpe pan, skillet, or griddle over medium-high heat (two pans will speed things up). Ladle about 1/3 cup (80 milliliters) batter onto the pan (do not oil it first); using the back of the ladle, immediately spread the batter in a circular motion from the center out to cover the pan and create a thin crêpe. (This is your test dosa; if it didn't spread easily, add some more water to the batter to thin it, and when you taste it, see if it needs a little more salt.)

When small holes form on the surface of the batter, drizzle a generous amount of oil over the dosa (putting the oil in a squeeze bottle makes this a lot easier) to help crisp it up. (Let me point out again that the oil gets added after the batter goes into the pan, not before; this inverse method of cooking crêpes often trips people up in the beginning.) When the bottom turns golden, about 1 minute, flip it over and cook on the other side for about 30 seconds, until lightly browned. Place the dosa on a serving plate and roll your choice of filling into it burrito style or fold it in half or quarters and serve with the filling alongside, using the dosa as your utensil. Wipe the pan with a dampened paper towel and continue making dosas with the remaining batter.

The Golden Dosa Rule

According to Nash, the first and most important rule of dosa making is to eat each dosa as soon as it comes off the pan, no waiting for your dining partners to be served. The dosa maker gets to sit down and eat only when his guests have had their fill. I've learned that bypassing the typical graces of serving a meal is really the way to go here, as dosas are best as soon as they are made; a few minutes later and they've lost their crispness. I particularly like this custom because Nash is the dedicated dosa maker in our house!

CHICKEN MASALA DOSA

Makes enough filling for 4 to 6 dosas

Some things take time and practice, and a good curry is one of them. The happy news is that once you've gotten a few techniques down, many curries follow a similar litany of steps: cooking the spices in oil until aromatic, browning onions in the spiced oil, then adding green chiles (the small killer spicy ones) and ginger-garlic paste, followed by some meat or vegetables and water or broth and setting the pot to simmer. In this dish the chicken is cooked separately and combined with the curry at the end for a fantastic marriage of flavors, inviting you to scoop it up with your freshly made dosas. (And if you haven't made dosas, this curry is equally good served over rice.) Thanks to my husband, Nash Patel, for his recipe.

2 pounds (900 grams) pastured dark chicken meat, cut into 2-inch (5-centimeter) pieces

1/4 cup (60 milliliters) yogurt, homemade (page 34) or store-bought (see Note)

1 to 2 teaspoons ground cayenne, to enjoyment level

1/2 teaspoon ground turmeric

1 1/2 teaspoons fine sea salt, plus more if needed

4 tablespoons extra-virgin olive oil or unrefined virgin coconut oil

4 whole cloves

4 cardamom pods

1 1/2-inch (4-centimeter) piece cinnamon stick

2 large red onions, chopped

1 to 8 small green chiles, to enjoyment level, seeded if you like, finely chopped

1 tablespoon ginger-garlic paste (see opposite)

1 teaspoon ground coriander

1 teaspoon ground cumin

1 (14.5-ounce/411-gram) can whole tomatoes with juices

1/2 teaspoon garam masala

1 cup (40 grams) chopped fresh cilantro

South Indian Lentil and Rice Dosas (page 152)

Green Yogurt Chutney (optional; see recipe opposite)

Put the chicken in a large bowl. Add the yogurt, cayenne, turmeric, and 3/4 teaspoon of the salt and stir well to coat the chicken or put on a disposable glove and massage the ingredients in with your hands. Cover and refrigerate for at least 1 hour or overnight (but not more, as overmarinated chicken can become mealy after cooking).

Heat 2 tablespoons of the oil in a large sauté pan over medium-high heat. Add the chicken and cook, stirring often, for about 15 minutes, until cooked through (it will be soupy). Pour the juices into a bowl or measuring cup, reduce the heat to medium, and continue to cook the chicken for about another 10 minutes, until browned.

While the chicken is cooking, make the onion and spice mixture: First, don't worry too much about the timing of the two pans; if the chicken is done before the onion and spice mixture or vice versa, leave one off the heat until the other is ready. Heat the remaining 2 tablespoons oil in a large sauté pan over medium-high heat. Add the cloves, cardamom, and cinnamon and cook for about 3 minutes, until aromatic. Add the onions and cook, stirring often, until fairly well browned, about 10 minutes.

Add the chiles and cook for about 2 minutes, until slightly softened. Add the ginger-garlic paste and cook for about 2 minutes, until the onion mixture is well browned, almost caramelized (pushing the boundary between sautéed and burnt is an important flavoring step). Add the coriander and cumin and cook, stirring, for 1 minute. Add the cooking liquid from the chicken and scrape up any browned bits from the bottom of the pan. Cook, stirring often, for about 5 minutes, until well thickened. Add the remaining ³/4 teaspoon salt and the tomatoes and cook, stirring to break up the tomatoes, for about 10 minutes.

Add the chicken to the tomatoes, then add the garam masala and cook for about 5 minutes to combine the flavors. Taste and season with more salt if needed. Stir in the cilantro and serve, either rolled into your dosas or alongside, using the dosa as utensil and with the chutney, if using, alongside.

NOTE: If you're not eating dairy, substitute 2 table-spoons rice vinegar for the yogurt and skip the chutney.

GREEN YOGURT CHUTNEY
Makes about ¹/2 cup (120 milliliters)

¹/2 small green chile, stem removed, halved, seeded if you like

3 cups (180 grams) fresh mint or cilantro leaves, or a mixture

About ¹/3 cup (80 milliliters) yogurt, homemade (page 34) or store-bought, plus more if needed

1¹/2 tablespoons fresh lime juice, or to taste

³/4 teaspoon unrefined sugar, or to taste

¹/2 teaspoon fine sea salt, or to taste

In a food processor or blender, combine all the ingredients and process until smooth, adding more yogurt as needed to reach a creamy consistency. Taste and add more lime juice, sugar, and/or salt if needed.

Homemade Ginger-Garlic Paste

This seasoning blend, indispensible in Indian cooking, is a refrigerator staple at my home. It is readily available at Indian groceries, but making your own is fresher and easy to accomplish: Combine equal amounts ginger and garlic in a food processor (a mini food processor if you have one) and process into a paste, adding just a little water if needed to get things moving. Store in the refrigerator for up to 1 month, or spoon little mounds of the paste onto a baking sheet lined with waxed paper, freeze the mounds, then pop them into a freezer bag for storage; remove them and use as needed. A quick alternative to the paste is to substitute equal parts finely minced garlic and ginger.

MOROCCAN-STYLE LAMB STEW
WITH PRUNES AND PRESERVED LEMON

FEATURED FERMENTS: **PRESERVED LEMON, GREEK YOGURT**

Serves 6

This dish highlights two favorite Moroccan ingredients: lamb, marinated in spices and cooked slowly to fall-apart tenderness, and preserved lemon, added near the end to give the stew a mildly tangy-salty flavor. Here the preserved lemon is cooked, so it's there primarily for flavor (and a very perky flavor it is!); a preserved lemon yogurt finishes the dish with a garnish of live culture. Serve over rice.

PRESERVED LEMON YOGURT

1 cup (240 milliliters) Greek yogurt, homemade (page 37) or store-bought

2 tablespoons minced Preserved Lemon peel (page 100)

1/4 cup (5 grams) finely chopped fresh mint

Pinch of fine sea salt

Pinch of freshly ground black pepper

LAMB STEW

2 1/2 pounds (1.25 kilograms) boneless pastured lamb shoulder or leg, cut into 2-inch (5-centimeter) pieces

3 tablespoons extra-virgin olive oil, plus more if needed

2 teaspoons mild paprika

2 teaspoons fine sea salt

1 teaspoon freshly ground black pepper

1 teaspoon ground cinnamon

1 teaspoon ground ginger

Pinch of saffron threads, crumbled

1 onion, chopped

3 tablespoons white wine

3 cups (720 milliliters) Traditional Broth (page 108), Vegetable Broth (page 109), or water

2 cups (8 ounces/230 grams) pitted prunes

1 Preserved Lemon, rinsed, pulp scooped out and discarded, peel thinly sliced

2 tablespoons unpasteurized honey

Make the preserved lemon yogurt: In a medium bowl, whisk together all the ingredients. Refrigerate while you prepare the lamb.

Make the lamb stew: Put the lamb in a heavy-duty zip-top bag. Pour the oil into a small bowl and stir in the paprika, salt, pepper, cinnamon, ginger, and saffron. Pour the spice mixture over the lamb, massaging it in from the outside of the bag, seal the bag, and marinate in the refrigerator for at least 1 hour or overnight.

Heat a medium Dutch oven over medium-high heat. Add the lamb in batches and sear on all sides, about 10 minutes, transfering the lamb to a bowl as each batch is done. Add the onion to the fat in the pan and cook for about 5 minutes, until softened. Add the wine and cook until almost evaporated, stirring to release the browned bits from the bottom of the pan.

Return the lamb to the pan, add the broth, bring to a simmer, then lower the heat, cover, and cook until the lamb is very tender, about 1 1/2 hours. Add the prunes and preserved lemon, briefly raise the heat to return to a simmer, then lower the heat, cover again, and cook for 20 minutes. Using a slotted spoon, transfer the lamb and prunes to a serving bowl. Increase the heat to high and boil until the juices are reduced to a medium sauce consistency, about 15 minutes. Add the honey and cook for another 5 minutes to give a little glaze to the sauce. Return the lamb and prunes to the pot and cook to heat through. Serve immediately, topped with the lemon yogurt.

PICKLED AND SMOTHERED PORK CHOPS

FEATURED FERMENTS: **PICKLE JUICE, JUICED-UP MUSTARD, COUNTERTOP CRÈME FRAÎCHE**

Serves 4

Pickle juice serves as our brine for a moist, tender, and infused-with-flavor chop. You can use pickle juice as the brine for other cuts of meat such as steak, chicken, and turkey, too; remember this and you'll never toss the juice from your pickle jar again! The chops are finished with mustard and crème fraîche for a cultured flourish, thanks to the superior flavors that fermentation brings to the plate. Serve with cultured applesauce and it will be over the top.

4 bone-in center-cut pastured pork chops, about 3/4 inch (2 centimeters) thick (about 1 1/2 pounds/680 grams)

About 2 cups (480 milliliters) pickle juice (page 29)

2 tablespoons extra-virgin olive oil, plus more for the pork chops

3 onions, thinly sliced

1/2 teaspoon fine sea salt, plus more if needed

1/2 teaspoon unrefined brown sugar

Splash of white wine

2 teaspoons Juiced-up Mustard (page 73)

1/2 teaspoon ground caraway seeds

1/4 cup (60 milliliters) Countertop Crème Fraîche (page 79), plus more for serving

1 tablespoon cultured butter (see page 53)

Freshly ground black pepper

Dill pickle spears (page 28; optional)

Put the pork chops in a nonreactive shallow bowl or container and pour pickle juice over them to cover. Cover and refrigerate for 8 to 24 hours to marinate.

Heat the oil in a large sauté pan over medium heat. Add the onions and salt and cook, stirring often, until very soft and starting to caramelize, about 20 minutes. Transfer the onions to a bowl, cover with a plate to keep them warm, and wipe the pan with a paper towel (rinse the pan if any onion bits are sticking to the pan).

Turn the heat under the sauté pan to medium-high and get it nice and hot. Remove the chops from the brine, discard the brine, and pat the chops dry with paper towels. Rub both sides with a small amount of oil to lightly coat. Sprinkle 1/8 teaspoon brown sugar on the meatier side of each chop. Add the chops to the pan (in batches if necessary), sugared side down, and cook for about 5 minutes, until lightly browned. Turn the chops, cover the pan, reduce the heat to low, and cook for another 3 to 4 minutes, until the chops are just cooked through and the internal temperature reads 145°F (62°C). Transfer the chops to a large plate to rest while you make the pan sauce.

Increase the heat under the pan to medium-high, add the wine, and stir to release any browned bits from the bottom. Remove from the heat and stir in the mustard and caraway seeds. Swirl in the crème fraîche followed by the butter, season with pepper and salt if needed, return the chops to the pan along with their juices, and turn to coat them in the sauce.

Divide the chops among serving plates and top with the onions and some crème fraîche. Serve with the pickle spears alongside if you like.

SUPERCHARGE: Serve with Tart and Crunchy Applesauce (page 182) and/or cornbread (see variation, page 170).

LEMONGRASS BEEF

FEATURED FERMENTS: **KOMBUCHA, MISO, FISH SAUCE, LIVE AND KICKIN' HOT SAUCE**

Serves 4

The mission of our featured ferments is to infuse the beef with flavor via marination and make it meltingly tender when it's cooked. The beef is then sliced and tossed with a liberal measure of Thai herbs and spices for a salty-tangy-umami salad experience.

BEEF

¼ cup (60 milliliters) unrefined sesame oil

¼ cup (60 milliliters) kombucha, homemade (page 44) or store-bought

3 tablespoons light or dark miso

¼ cup (60 milliliters) fish sauce

2 tablespoons fresh lime juice

2 tablespoons Live and Kickin' Hot Sauce (page 81)

2 fresh lemongrass stalks, tender bottom parts only, thinly sliced then ground to a paste with about 1 tablespoon water in a spice grinder (set aside 1 tablespoon before grinding for the salad)

3 garlic cloves, pressed through a garlic press

1 (1½-pound/680-gram) boneless beef sirloin steak (about 1 inch/2.5 centimeters thick)

1 tablespoon unrefined virgin coconut oil

SALAD

4 large shallots, sliced into thin rings

3 tablespoons fresh lime juice

3 tablespoons fish sauce

½ cup (20 grams) chopped fresh mint

½ cup (20 grams) chopped fresh cilantro

½ cup (50 grams) mung bean sprouts (optional)

1 tablespoon reserved minced fresh lemongrass

1 tablespoon raw white rice plus 2 dried red chiles, toasted and ground (see Note)

FOR SERVING

Hot rice, such as sticky rice

Lime wedges, fish sauce, Live and Kickin' Hot Sauce

Make the beef: In a medium bowl, whisk together the sesame oil, kombucha, miso, fish sauce, lime juice, hot sauce, lemongrass, and garlic. Put the beef in a heavy-duty zip-top bag, add the marinade, seal the bag, and massage the marinade into the meat. Refrigerate for at least 2 hours or up to 24 hours to fully infuse the beef with lemongrass flavor.

Remove the beef from the marinade and remove most of the marinade. Heat a large cast-iron skillet over medium-high heat for about 5 minutes, until very hot. Add the coconut oil to the pan and swirl to melt it, then add the steak and resist touching it for 3 to 4 minutes to create a nice crust, then flip it and cook for another 3 to 4 minutes. Place the steak on a cutting board, let rest for about 5 minutes, then thinly slice it.

Make the salad: Put the steak in a large bowl. Add the shallots, lime juice, fish sauce, mint, cilantro, bean sprouts, if using, lemongrass, and toasted ground rice and chiles and toss to coat. Serve over rice with lime wedges, fish sauce, and hot sauce to pass at the table.

NOTE: Toast the rice and chiles in a small skillet over medium heat for about 2 minutes, until aromatic and just starting to color. Cool slightly, then grind to a coarse powder in a spice grinder.

MEXICAN PORK STEW WITH SALSA VERDE

FEATURED FERMENT AND OPTIONS: SALSA VERDE, SALSA ALIVE, LIVE AND KICKIN'
HOT SAUCE, GUACAMOLE WITH A KICK, COUNTERTOP CRÈME FRAÎCHE

Serves 6 to 8

This recipe reminds us that many a dish is enhanced with a fermented finish, in this case a liberal slathering of salsa verde. And you needn't stop there; see below for more cultured options to add to this Mexican comfort food classic.

3 pounds (1.4 kilograms) boneless pastured pork shoulder, trimmed and cut into 1-inch (2.5-centimeter) cubes

2 large fresh chorizo sausages, casings removed

2 white onions, sliced

3 garlic cloves, chopped

1 (28-ounce/800-gram) can whole tomatoes with juices

½ (7-ounce/199-gram) can chipotle chiles in adobo sauce, finely chopped

1 teaspoon dried oregano

1 teaspoon dried thyme

1½ teaspoons fine sea salt

½ bunch fresh cilantro, leaves and tender stems, chopped

Salsa Verde (page 75)

Optional toppings: Salsa Alive (page 76), Live and Kickin' Hot Sauce (page 81), Guacamole with a Kick (page 116), Countertop Crème Fraîche (page 79)

Accompaniments: Rice or warmed corn tortillas, such as Ezekiel brand sprouted corn tortillas, sliced avocado, and red onion and radish slices

Heat a large saucepan over medium-high heat. Add half of the pork shoulder and brown it all over, stirring a few times, about 10 minutes. Transfer the pork shoulder to a bowl. Add the remaining pork shoulder to the pan and brown it in the same way, then transfer it to the bowl. Reduce the heat to medium, add the chorizo to the pan, and cook, stirring to break it up, until cooked through, about 10 minutes. Transfer the chorizo to the bowl with the pork shoulder. Add the onions to the fat in the pan and cook, stirring often, until softened and starting to brown. Add the garlic and cook for 2 minutes, or until softened.

Pour about ¼ cup (60 milliliters) of the tomato juice from the can into the pan and stir to release any browned bits from the bottom of the pan. Return the pork shoulder and chorizo to the pan. Add the chipotle chiles with their sauce, the oregano, thyme, and salt to the pan. Crush the tomatoes directly into the pan and add the remaining juices from the can.

Cover, bring to a simmer, then reduce the heat to low and cook, stirring occasionally, for about 2 hours, until the meat is fall-apart tender. Mash the pork directly in the pan with a potato masher; it should break apart easily. Stir in the cilantro and serve with salsa verde and any other toppings and accompaniments you choose. If you're making tacos, serve the pork with a slotted spoon to keep your tortillas from getting soggy.

CHAPTER SIX

DESSERTS

CHOCOLATE AVOCADO MOUSSE
WITH COCONUT KEFIR CREAM

FEATURED FERMENT: **COCONUT KEFIR CREAM**

———

Serves 4

Avocado is working its way into the world of desserts, and it makes perfect sense because the velvety nature and mild flavor of this fruit (yes, avocado is a fruit) make it a perfect starting point for dairy-free cream-based sweet treats. Coconut Kefir Cream furthers the richness of this dessert; dollop a little more of the cream on top as a crowning touch.

2 ripe Hass avocados, halved, pitted, flesh scooped out

1/2 cup (120 milliliters) Coconut Kefir Cream (see recipe opposite), plus more for topping

1/2 cup (40 grams) unsweetened cocoa powder

1/2 cup (100 grams) packed dark brown sugar

1 tablespoon fresh lemon juice

1 teaspoon pure vanilla extract

Large pinch of fine sea salt

In a food processor, combine all the ingredients and process until silky smooth, 3 to 4 minutes (see Note), scraping the sides of the machine once or twice, as needed.

　　Spoon into bowls and serve with a dollop of Coconut Kefir Cream. The mousse will keep, covered and refrigerated, for 2 to 3 days.

NOTE: Processing takes a while to achieve best results—in a minute or two you'll arrive at creamy, but don't stop there; the full amount of time gets you to silky smooth, what we're looking for in a mousse.

VARIATIONS

Any number of flavorings will add variety to your mousse; the rule of thumb is to use concentrated flavorings in small amounts so your mousse stays thick. These are two favorites:

ORANGE CHOCOLATE AVOCADO MOUSSE:
Add 1 tablespoon Grand Marnier.

ALMOND CHOCOLATE AVOCADO MOUSSE: Add 2 teaspoons amaretto or 1 teaspoon almond extract.

SWAPS: Make your mousse with Coconut Milk Kefir (page 41) instead of Coconut Kefir Cream to save the step of separating out the cream.

　　Substitute Countertop Crème Fraîche (page 79) for the Coconut Kefir Cream for those who enjoy dairy.

COCONUT KEFIR CREAM

Makes about 2 cups (480 milliliters)

This rich and slightly tangy cultured dessert topping is a type of kefir made from the creamy part of coconut milk from the can. It can be used where you'd use dairy whipped cream or crème fraîche. It's the base of my Ginger Plum Fool (page 167), and a dollop could finish any of the dessert recipes that follow. It's also a topping for pancakes (page 56) or waffles and is perfect spooned over a simple bowl of berries.

2 (13.5-ounce/398-milliliter) cans coconut milk, or 2 (5.4-ounce/160-milliliter) cans unsweetened coconut cream

¼ cup (60 milliliters) Coconut Water Kefir (page 41) or Water Kefir (page 42)

Organic confectioners' sugar or maple syrup to taste

½ teaspoon pure vanilla extract (optional)

If using coconut milk (see Notes), refrigerate the cans for 6 to 8 hours and remove without opening or shaking them. Turn the cans upside down, open the tops, and pour the liquid part of the coconut milk into a jar and save it for another use (see Notes). Spoon the coconut cream into a blender, add the Coconut Water Kefir, and blend until smooth. Transfer to a glass container, cover loosely, and set aside to ferment at room temperature for 12 to 24 hours, until pleasantly tangy smelling and tasting. (See page 41 for more detailed instructions on making coconut kefir.) Cover and refrigerate until cold.

Place the coconut kefir cream in a large bowl. Taste it to see how tangy it is. If you like it as-is, no sweetener is required. If you'd like it a little sweet, add confectioners' sugar or maple syrup to taste. Add the vanilla, if using. Using a whisk, beat the cream (see Notes) for about 20 seconds, until it's smooth and forms stiff peaks. Use immediately or cover and refrigerate until ready to use; give it a few good turns of the whisk before serving.

NOTES: If you are using coconut cream, there's no need to refrigerate; just open the can and scoop out the cream.

You'll only need the solidified coconut for the whipped cream. Save the liquid for a shake or smoothie. Or why not culture it? Just follow the directions for making Coconut Water Kefir (page 41).

If the cream is to be blended into a recipe (as in the mousse) rather than getting dolloped on top, there's no need to whip it before using.

GINGER PLUM FOOL

FEATURED FERMENT: **COCONUT KEFIR CREAM**

Serves 4

Fool is a classic British dessert of pureed fruit folded into whipped cream; here in this loose interpretation of the fool, I use Coconut Kefir Cream to make it dairy free and full of the richness, probiotics, and healthy fats found in coconut kefir. Once you've made the cream and plums it's a very easy dessert to put together and can be assembled right before serving. Peaches or apricots could be substituted for the plums.

1 pound (450 grams) plums, pitted and sliced

¼ cup (60 milliliters) maple syrup

1 tablespoon grated fresh ginger

1¼ cups (300 milliliters) Coconut Kefir Cream (page 165)

Minced crystallized ginger (optional)

Combine the plums, maple syrup, and ginger in a medium saucepan. Place over medium heat and bring to a simmer, stirring, then continue to cook until the plums break down to a chunky mixture and the syrup that forms starts to thicken, about 15 minutes. Transfer to a bowl and cool completely, then cover and refrigerate until cold.

Divide the plum mixture among four dessert bowls. Fold the coconut kefir cream into the plums in a haphazard fashion, leaving streaks of cream throughout the plums. Garnish with a little crystallized ginger if you like and serve immediately.

SWAPS: Substitute 1 cup (240 milliliters) Countertop Crème Fraîche (page 79), whipped to soft peaks, for the Coconut Kefir Cream.

Make your fool using Tipsy Fruit (page 60) instead of the plum compote.

STRAWBERRY AND COINTREAU ICE CREAM

FEATURED FERMENT: **DAIRY KEFIR**

Makes a little more than 1 quart (1 liter)

Kefir ice cream is a new frontier in the world of frozen desserts: light, lively, slightly tart, and full of probiotic goodness, as long as you don't heat the kefir as you would the standard dairy to make a typical ice cream custard base. (Unlike cooking, freezing doesn't kill the good bacteria.) To accomplish this, I make a custard with the cream and egg yolks and add the kefir after the custard has cooled, thus ensuring that those good bacteria in the kefir keep their potency.

Here sweet, juicy strawberries make a fruity companion to frozen kefir, and a few splashes of Cointreau add a happy hint of orange. Those avoiding alcohol can omit the Cointreau or substitute a splash of orange flower water. You might top off a bowl with a little strawberry jam and a dollop of Coconut Kefir Cream (page 165), though I must confess my favorite topping is rainbow sprinkles (I buy the all-natural brand from my co-op, colored with turmeric, cabbage, and annatto): sweet, colorful, and whimsical set against a scoop of the strawberry-pink ice cream.

If you don't have an ice cream maker, see the sidebar for options for making your ice cream without one.

1 cup (240 milliliters) heavy cream

2 large egg yolks

1 cup (240 grams) unrefined cane sugar

2 cups (480 milliliters) dairy kefir (page 39; see Note)

Pinch of sea salt

1 quart fresh strawberries (about 1 pound/450 grams), hulled and halved

2 tablespoons fresh lemon juice

1/2 cup (120 milliliters) Cointreau

Put the cream in a medium heavy-bottomed saucepan. Place over medium-low heat and heat until tiny bubbles start to form around the edges and the mixture reaches 160°F (70°C) as measured on an instant-read thermometer.

Meanwhile, in a medium heatproof bowl, whisk the egg yolks until smooth. Slowly whisk in 3/4 cup (180 grams) of the sugar until it is well incorporated and the mixture is thick and pale yellow. Temper the egg yolks by very slowly pouring in the hot cream while whisking continuously. Return the custard to the saucepan and place over low heat. Heat, stirring frequently, until the custard looks silky, is thick enough to coat the back of the spoon, and reaches a temperature of 175°F (80°C). Do not allow the mixture to boil.

Pour the mixture through a fine-mesh strainer into a clean bowl and let cool to room temperature, stirring occasionally. To cool the mixture quickly, set the bowl in a larger bowl filled with ice and water and stir often until cooled. Once cooled, add the kefir and salt, cover, and refrigerate the ice cream base until cold, at least 2 hours or overnight.

Meanwhile, combine the strawberries with the remaining ¼ cup (60 grams) sugar and the lemon juice in a medium saucepan and toss to dissolve the sugar. Let sit for 20 minutes to macerate, stirring occasionally.

Add the Cointreau to the pan, place the pan over medium-low heat, and cook, stirring to break up the strawberries a bit, until the strawberries soften and a syrup forms and starts to thicken, about 30 minutes. Remove from the heat, transfer to a container, and cool to room temperature. Cover and refrigerate until cold, at least 2 hours or overnight.

Remove the ice cream base from the refrigerator, pour it into a blender, add three quarters of the strawberries and their syrup, and blend until fully incorporated.

Pour the mixture into the frozen container of an ice cream machine and churn according to the manufacturer's instructions, adding the reserved strawberries 5 minutes before the churning is finished. Transfer to an airtight container and freeze for at least 2 hours before serving.

NOTE: Those new to kefir might start with a smaller amount of kefir, perhaps 1 cup (240 milliliters), and increase the heavy cream to 2 cups (480 milliliters).

Ice Cream Without an Ice Cream Machine

It's possible to make ice cream (and sorbet, too) without an ice cream machine; all that's needed is a food processor or a simple baking pan, some cleared-out space in your freezer, and a little at-home time. Your ice cream may be slightly less creamy than that made in a machine, but it will be pretty darn close.

In a food processor: Pour the cold ice cream base into the bowl of a food processor, place in the freezer, and freeze for 1 hour. Take the bowl out and scrape the frozen mixture from the sides of the bowl. Run the food processor for a few seconds. Scrape the sides again and run the machine for a few more seconds. Return the bowl to the freezer and freeze again. Repeat, now freezing for 30 minutes at a time and processing and scraping, until a very soft ice cream is formed, 3 to 4 hours total. Transfer the ice cream to a freezer-safe container and freeze until fairly firm, at least 4 hours or overnight.

In a baking pan: Pour the cold ice cream base into an 8-inch (20-centimeter) baking dish, place in the freezer, and freeze for 1 hour. Take it out, scrape the mixture from the sides of the pan, and vigorously whisk with a hand whisk or immersion blender. Return the pan to the freezer and freeze again. Repeat, now freezing for 30 minutes at a time and whisking and scraping, until a very soft ice cream is formed, 3 to 4 hours total. Transfer the ice cream to a freezer-safe container and freeze until fairly firm, at least 4 hours or overnight.

CARDAMOM CORN CAKE

FEATURED FERMENTS: **BUTTERMILK, COUNTERTOP CRÈME FRAÎCHE**

Makes one 9-inch (23-centimeter) cake

Using corn flour rather than the typical cornmeal that goes into cornbread lends this cake a smooth, light, and airy crumb. (If you don't have corn flour on hand, you can make a reasonable substitute by whizzing cornmeal in a blender until it reaches a fine, floury consistency.) It's flavored lightly with honey, rather than going birthday-cake sweet, making it a perfect companion to afternoon tea.

2¹/₂ cups (300 grams) fine corn flour

1 teaspoon baking powder

1 teaspoon baking soda

1¹/₄ teaspoons ground cardamom

¹/₂ teaspoon fine sea salt

2 large farm-fresh eggs

2 cups (480 milliliters) buttermilk (see page 36)

12 tablespoons (90 milliliters) light liquid honey

3 teaspoons pure vanilla extract

¹/₂ cup (1 stick/115 grams) unsalted butter,
    cut into pieces

2 cups (480 milliliters) Countertop Crème Fraîche
    (page 79), well chilled

Sweetened shredded coconut (optional)

Preheat the oven to 375°F (190°C) and set an oven rack in the middle position.

In a large bowl, whisk together the corn flour, baking powder, baking soda, cardamom, and salt. In a separate bowl, beat the eggs, then whisk in the buttermilk, 7 tablespoons of the honey, and 1 teaspoon of the vanilla. Add the wet ingredients to the dry ingredients and whisk just until blended. Put the butter in a 10-inch (25-centimeter) cast-iron skillet and place in the oven until the butter melts. Remove the skillet from the oven and pour all but 1 tablespoon of the butter into the batter, gently folding it in.

Pour the batter into the skillet and bake for 25 to 30 minutes, until the edges start to brown, the top begins to crack, and a toothpick inserted in the center comes out clean. Turn out onto a wire rack and let cool completely.

Using a serrated knife, split the cake horizontally into two layers and place each layer on a plate, cut side up. Place 2 tablespoons of the remaining honey in a small saucepan, add 2 tablespoons water, and heat to dissolve the honey. Brush the honey on the cut sides of both cake layers.

Put the crème fraîche in the bowl of an electric mixer, add the remaining 3 tablespoons honey and the remaining 2 teaspoons vanilla, and beat on medium speed until soft peaks form. Spread half of the filling over the cut side of the bottom corn cake layer, top with the second layer, cut side down, and frost the top with the remaining frosting. Decorate the top with a garnish of coconut if you like.

The cake is best eaten the day it's made. If you're planning on eating just a slice or two at a time, just serve the slices whole, drizzling each slice with some honey and topping with the whipped crème fraîche. Wrap what's left in plastic, refrigerate, and toast leftover slices the next day; spread the slices with more whipped crème fraîche, butter, or jam.

VARIATION

SAVORY CORNBREAD: Omit the cardamom and honey and skip the frosting.

LEMON AND TART DRIED CHERRY CRÈME FRAÎCHE ICE CREAM

FEATURED FERMENT: **COUNTERTOP CRÈME FRAÎCHE**

———

Makes a little more than 1 quart (1 liter)

This frozen dessert features the subtle sourness of crème fraîche, puckery lemon, and tart dried cherries. You can omit the cherries for a pure lemon experience. If you don't have an ice cream maker, see page 169 for information about making your ice cream without one.

2 cups (480 milliliters) heavy cream

2 large egg yolks

3/4 to 1 cup (180 to 240 grams) unrefined cane sugar, depending on how tangy your crème fraîche is

2 cups (480 milliliters) Countertop Crème Fraîche (page 79)

6 tablespoons (90 milliliters) fresh lemon juice

Pinch of fine sea salt

2/3 cup (100 grams) sweetened or unsweetened dried cherries, soaked in water to cover for 2 hours and drained

Put the heavy cream in a medium heavy-bottomed saucepan. Place over medium-low heat and heat until tiny bubbles start to form around the edges and the mixture reaches 160°F (70°C) as measured on an instant-read thermometer.

Meanwhile, in a medium heatproof bowl, whisk the egg yolks until smooth. Slowly whisk in the sugar until it is well incorporated and the mixture is thick and pale yellow. Temper the egg yolks by very slowly pouring in the hot cream while whisking continuously. Return the custard to the saucepan and place over low heat. Heat, stirring frequently, until the custard looks silky, is thick enough to coat the back of the spoon, and reaches a temperature of 175°F (80°C). Do not allow the mixture to boil.

Pour the mixture through a fine-mesh strainer into a clean bowl and let cool to room temperature, stirring occasionally. To cool the mixture quickly, set the bowl in a larger bowl filled with ice and water and stir often until cooled. Once cooled, whisk in the crème fraîche, lemon juice, and salt, cover, and refrigerate until cold, at least 2 hours or overnight.

Pour the mixture into the frozen container of an ice cream machine and churn according to the manufacturer's instructions, adding the dried cherries 5 minutes before the churning is finished. Transfer to an airtight container and freeze for at least 2 hours before serving.

REAL-DEAL BLUEBERRY FROZEN YOGURT

FEATURED FERMENT: **YOGURT**

Makes about 1 quart (1 liter)

Real frozen yogurt is creamy, tangy, and full-bodied and contains few ingredients other than pure yogurt and something to sweeten and flavor it naturally. Though the fro-yo business has become a multimillion-dollar affair, many products on the market are little more than junk food, loaded with hard-to-pronounce ingredients and unwholesome sweeteners and lacking in probiotic profile (and then you top them with gummy bears).

Homemade frozen yogurt will taste like the yogurt that went into it; make your own or use a good-quality brand for a truly cultured frozen dessert. If you don't have an ice cream maker, see page 169 for information about making your frozen yogurt without one.

3 cups (440 grams) fresh blueberries

2/3 cup (160 milliliters) unpasteurized honey, or to taste

3 tablespoons fresh lemon juice

Pinch of fine sea salt

3 cups (720 milliliters) yogurt, homemade (page 34) or store-bought

Combine the blueberries, honey, and lemon juice in a medium saucepan. Place over medium-low heat and cook until the blueberries pop and soften and the syrup that forms starts to thicken, about 10 minutes. Remove from the heat, add the salt, and cool to room temperature. Transfer to a blender, add the yogurt, and blend until fully incorporated. Taste and add more honey if needed, keeping in mind that your frozen yogurt will taste less sweet once frozen. Place in a container, cover, and refrigerate until cold, at least 2 hours. You can prepare the base a day ahead.

Pour the mixture into the frozen container of an ice cream machine and churn according to the manufacturer's instructions. Transfer to an airtight container and freeze for at least 2 hours before serving.

VARIATION
BLUEBERRY AND ROSEWATER FROZEN YOGURT: Add 2 teaspoons rosewater to the custard before churning.

TANGY COCONUT SORBET

FEATURED FERMENT: **COCONUT MILK KEFIR**

―――――

Makes 1 quart (1 liter)

Heavenly rich cultured coconut milk makes for a sorbet that's both creamy and slightly tangy. Coconut cultures are some of the easiest to make at home, as they can be set up in seconds (patience is required only while your coconut ferments on the counter overnight), making this dessert doable for both dedicated DIY fermenters and those just dabbling in the craft of culturing. The rum is included here for flavor, yes, but it also helps to keep the sorbet smooth by preventing the formation of ice crystals. It can be omitted for those avoiding alcohol.

One of the things I like most about making frozen cultured desserts is that every batch will be unique, based on the amount of culture you use, how long you've fermented it, and the individual nature of your starter's bacteria. Sometimes it will be a little more tart, sometimes a little sweeter. Taste your kefir, and use the larger quantity of sugar if it's especially tangy, keeping in mind that your sorbet or ice cream will taste less sweet once frozen.

If you don't have an ice cream maker, see page 169 for information about making your sorbet without one.

2/3 to 3/4 cup (80 to 180 grams) unrefined sugar

2 cups (480 milliliters) cold Coconut Milk Kefir (page 41)

1 tablespoon coconut rum or other light rum (optional)

1/3 cup (30 grams) fresh shredded or desiccated coconut (optional)

In a medium saucepan, combine 1 cup (240 milliliters) water and the sugar, place over medium heat, and bring to a simmer. Simmer for about 5 minutes, until the sugar has dissolved. Cool to room temperature, pour into a container, and refrigerate until cold, about 2 hours. Whisk in the coconut milk kefir, add the rum, if using, pour the mixture into the frozen container of an ice cream machine, and churn according to the manufacturer's instructions; if using the shredded coconut, add it 5 minutes before the churning is completed. Transfer to an airtight container and freeze for at least 2 hours before serving.

SALTY MOLASSES COCONUT SORBET
Makes 1 quart (1 liter)

A bold-tasting variation on the cultured coconut sorbet, for lovers of the salty-sweet flavor combination.

1/4 cup (60 milliliters) unsulfured molasses

1/4 cup (60 milliliters) hot water

2 cups (480 milliliters) cold Coconut Milk Kefir (page 41)

1/4 cup (60 milliliters) maple syrup

1 tablespoon cognac or bourbon (optional)

1/2 teaspoon fine sea salt

In a large bowl, whisk the molasses with the hot water. Whisk in the coconut milk kefir, maple syrup, cognac, if using, and salt. Pour the mixture into the frozen container of an ice cream machine and churn according to the manufacturer's instructions. Transfer to an airtight container and freeze for at least 2 hours before serving.

FROM TOP: Raspberry-Lime Granita (page 176), Tangy Coconut Sorbet, and Real-Deal Blueberry Frozen Yogurt (page 173).

RASPBERRY-LIME GRANITA

Makes about 1 quart (1 liter)

Granita, a semifrozen dessert originally hailing from Sicily, is like an upscale version of Italian ice or a light, flaky version of sorbet. The typical base is water, sugar, and fruit or other flavorings. Here I've swapped in Coconut Water Kefir for the plain water and honey for the sugar, making this version simultaneously less refined and more cultured than a traditional granita. A generous amount of raspberry puree lends a surprising creaminess to the granita, with the effect of both quenching your thirst and providing a sense of satiation. A parfait glass with alternate layers of Coconut Kefir Cream (page 165) or Countertop Crème Fraîche (page 79) would further that effect.

1 quart (500 grams) fresh or thawed frozen raspberries

¼ cup (60 milliliters) fresh lime juice

1½ cups (360 milliliters) Coconut Water Kefir (page 41)

⅔ cup (160 milliliters) unpasteurized light honey, such as orange blossom or clover, or to taste

½ teaspoon pure vanilla extract

Pinch of fine sea salt

2 teaspoons finely grated lime zest

Fresh mint leaves

Combine the raspberries and lime juice in a food processor and process until smooth. If you prefer your granita seedless, pour into a fine-mesh strainer placed over a bowl, pressing on the solids to extract the raspberry puree. Discard the seeds. If you like the crunch of seeds in your granita, simply pour the pureed raspberries into a bowl. Add the kefir, honey, vanilla, and salt and whisk to dissolve the honey. Whisk in the lime zest.

Pour the mixture into a 9-inch (23-centimeter) square baking dish and place in the freezer. Freeze until icy around the edges, about 40 minutes. Using a fork, stir the icy parts into the middle of the pan. Continue stirring the edges into the center every 20 to 30 minutes for about 3 hours, until the granita is almost completely frozen and the texture is similar to shaved ice. To serve, scrape the surface of the granita with a fork to create shaved ice crystals. Scoop into dessert glasses, garnish with mint leaves, and serve immediately. You can make the granita ahead of time; thaw slightly and give it a quick scrape before serving.

SWAP: Substitute Water Kefir (page 42) for the Coconut Water Kefir.

KOMBUCHA GRANITA

Makes about 1 quart (1 liter)

Kombucha granita is sweet relief from the heat of the summer, and the beauty of the recipe is that it takes almost no time to make, especially if you use a great store-bought kombucha brand. It's also endlessly adaptable—see my suggestions below on flavoring your granita.

2 cups (480 milliliters) kombucha, plain or your choice of flavor, homemade (page 44) or store-bought

Maple syrup, unpasteurized honey, or other sweetener of choice (optional; see Note)

Pour the kombucha into a 9-inch (23-centimeter) square baking dish, whisk in the maple syrup, if using, and place in the freezer. Freeze until icy around the edges, about 30 minutes. Using a fork, stir the icy parts into the middle of the pan. Continue stirring the edges into the center every 20 to 30 minutes for about 2 hours, until the granita is almost completely frozen and the texture is similar to shaved ice.

To serve, scrape the surface of the granita with a fork to create shaved ice crystals. Scoop into dessert glasses and serve immediately. You can make the granita ahead of time; thaw it slightly and give it a quick scrape before serving.

NOTE: The perception of sweetness is lessened when a food is frozen, so you might want to make your granita base a little sweeter than you would make a beverage.

Kombucha Slush and Other Granita Variations

The first time I made a kombucha granita, I opened a bottle of High Country Wild Root Kombucha, stirred in a little maple syrup for good measure (my friends later spiked theirs with maple liqueur), and froze it as described above. The result: a lively root beer slush, refreshing scooped from a bowl or, for a special treat, poured into a glass and mixed with a scoop of vanilla ice cream and melted into an icy kombucha root beer float.

Other granita flavoring ideas:

Kombucha Lemonade Granita: Add lemon or lime juice.

Kombucha Ginger Beer Granita: Add juice squeezed from freshly grated ginger.

Grapefruit Kombucha Granita: Use half grapefruit juice; try it as a palate cleanser.

Vanilla and Rosewater Kombucha Granita: Add vanilla extract and rosewater.

DEVILISH CUPCAKES

FEATURED FERMENTS: **BUTTERMILK, COUNTERTOP CRÈME FRAÎCHE**

Makes 12

These double-chocolate cupcakes are courtesy of my good friend, the talented pastry chef Patricia Austin, who runs Wild Flour Vermont Bakery (wildflourbakeryvt.com), a French-inspired farmers' market bakery based in Brattleboro, Vermont. Next time you're in the area, stop by the market on a Saturday and be prepared to be dazzled.

CUPCAKES

1 cup (115 grams) gluten-free flour mix, preferably Authentic Foods brand GF Classical Blend

½ teaspoon baking powder

½ teaspoon finely ground chia seeds (see Note)

¼ teaspoon fine sea salt

6 tablespoons (90 milliliters) boiling water

6 tablespoons (45 grams) unsweetened Dutch-processed cocoa powder

½ cup (120 milliliters) buttermilk, homemade (see sidebar, page 36) or store-bought

¾ teaspoon baking soda

4 tablespoons (½ stick/55 grams) unsalted butter, at room temperature

1 cup (240 grams) sugar

1 teaspoon pure vanilla extract

1 large farm-fresh egg

GANACHE (MAKES 2 CUPS/80 MILLILITERS)

8 ounces (300 grams) dark chocolate, chopped into ¼-inch (6-millimeter) pieces

1 cup (240 milliliters) Countertop Crème Fraîche (page 79)

Make the cupcakes: Preheat the oven to 350°F (175°C) and line a 12-cup muffin pan with paper liners.

Sift the flour mix, baking powder, chia seeds, and salt into a large bowl. In a separate bowl, combine the boiling water and cocoa powder and whisk until the mixture is smooth and homogenous. Set aside.

Pour the buttermilk into a generously sized bowl, leaving room for possible expansion. Put the baking soda in a small bowl and set both the buttermilk and baking soda aside.

Combine the butter, sugar, and vanilla in the bowl of an electric mixer fitted with the paddle attachment. Beat on high speed until the ingredients are creamed (lightened in color and fluffy), about 3 minutes. Add the egg and beat on high speed for about 1 minute. Scrape the inside of the bowl and beat again briefly.

Add the baking soda to the buttermilk, stirring thoroughly with a rubber spatula; the mixture may foam and expand.

With the mixer off, add one third of the flour mixture to the butter mixture and beat on low speed until the ingredients are just incorporated. Add one third of the buttermilk mixture and continue adding the flour mixture and buttermilk in this fashion, beating on medium-low speed until all the ingredients are added. Scrape the inside of the bowl and beat until the batter is smooth.

Add the cocoa mixture and beat until the batter is uniform in color and texture. Remove the bowl from the mixer and, using a rubber spatula, finish mixing the batter by hand, making sure to scrape the insides and bottom of the bowl.

Fill the muffin cups three-quarters full with batter. Bake for 20 minutes, or until the cupcakes spring back when gently touched at the center. Remove from the oven and place on a wire rack to cool for 10 minutes, then remove them from the pan and cool completely on the rack.

While the cupcakes are cooling, make the ganache: Put the chocolate in a medium stainless-steel bowl that will fit snugly inside a saucepan.

Pour a few inches of water into the saucepan and bring to a simmer over medium-low heat. Set the bowl of chocolate on top of the simmering water; make sure the water is not touching the bottom of the bowl. Stir the chocolate with a rubber spatula until it has melted fully, about 5 minutes.

Remove the chocolate from the heat and add half of the crème fraîche, whisking it gently into the melted chocolate in a slow circular motion. Add the remaining crème fraîche and stir to combine, taking your time to allow the two ingredients to emulsify and create a smooth, thick ganache. (The density of ganache can be changed by adjusting the proportions of chocolate and crème fraîche. More chocolate makes a thicker ganache, while more crème fraîche gives a thinner consistency. Another method of thinning ganache is to add small amounts of water until you reach the desired consistency.)

Immediately frost the cupcakes with the ganache. Or if you're not ready to frost them, place plastic wrap directly onto the surface of the ganache and transfer to the refrigerator, where it will keep for up to 2 weeks. When you are ready to use the ganache, allow it to sit at room temperature for 30 minutes, or until it has softened to a workable consistency. If necessary, gently stir or whisk the ganache to ensure a creamy, homogenous consistency.

NOTE: Ground chia seeds are used in this recipe as a replacement for xanthan gum. Xanthan gum is used in gluten-free baking to help stand in for the role of gluten; however, it is known to cause gastric upset in many individuals. The egg helps bind and the chia seeds give additional support to the batter and finished cupcakes by helping to thicken, bind, and provide structure. Chia seeds are also a superfood: Every seed is a complete protein and is packed with omega-3 fatty acids, fiber, and antioxidants.

SPARKLING BERRY SALAD

FEATURED FERMENT: **KOMBUCHA**

———

Serves 4

This simple dessert gets better the longer the fruit soaks in the tangy maple syrup–sweetened kombucha marinade. Just about any fruit will be delicious steeped in kombucha, so feel free to vary your ingredients according to what's in season. You can play with your flavors, too, adding a little cinnamon, vanilla extract, rosewater, or orange flower water, for example—anything that matches the flavor of kombucha and variety of fruit you're using. A dollop of Coconut Kefir Cream or Crème Fraîche at the end makes it extra-special, as would a scoop of any of the frozen desserts in this chapter (pages 168 and 172 through 177).

1 quart (500 grams) mixed berries, such as blueberries, blackberries, raspberries, and halved strawberries, or just one kind

2 cups (480 milliliters) kombucha, homemade (page 44) or store-bought, any flavor

Maple syrup

Coconut Kefir Cream (page 165) or Countertop Crème Fraîche (page 79; optional)

Fresh mint sprigs

Put the berries in a medium bowl or container. Add the kombucha and stir. Taste and sweeten with maple syrup, a little if your kombucha and fruit are starting off sweet; more if your ingredients are tangy. Stir well to dissolve the maple syrup. Cover and refrigerate for at least 1 hour or overnight.

Scoop the berries from the juices into bowls, including as much or as little of the juice in your servings as you like. (If you have a good amount of juice left over, you could do another round of maceration with additional fruit.) Top with coconut kefir cream or crème fraîche if you like and serve, topping each bowl with a mint sprig.

STAR ANISE-SPICED APPLE CRUMBLE

FEATURED FERMENT: **TART AND CRUNCHY APPLESAUCE**

Serves 10 to 12

This crumble is live and dairy free, made with an uncooked almond and date crust and a fragrant cultured applesauce filling. It calls out for a creamy topping, either Coconut Kefir Cream or coconut sorbet, to complete it. The crust can be made a day ahead of time; you might time it so the crust is ready and waiting when the filling has fermented to your liking.

DATE-NUT CRUST

3 cups (420 grams) almonds (see Note)

9 dates, pitted, halved, soaked in water for 1 hour, and drained

2 tablespoons unpasteurized honey

1 teaspoon pure vanilla extract

¼ teaspoon fine sea salt

APPLESAUCE FILLING

1 recipe Tart and Crunchy Applesauce (page 182)

TOPPING

Unpasteurized honey, for drizzling (optional; use if your applesauce is on the tangy side or to satisfy a sweet tooth)

Dollops of Coconut Kefir Cream (page 165; optional)

Scoops of Tangy Coconut Sorbet (page 174; optional)

Make the date-nut crust: Combine the almonds, dates, honey, vanilla, and salt in a food processor and pulse to form a coarse, sticky puree (don't overprocess or it will turn to nut butter). Press about two-thirds of the mixture into a 9-by-13-inch (23-by-33-centimeter) baking dish to make a crust, reserving the rest to sprinkle over the crumble.

Make the applesauce filling: Spoon the applesauce into a fine-mesh strainer set over a large bowl. Press on the solids to extract most of the liquid. Reserve the liquid (see Supercharge, below).

Spread the applesauce filling over the crust and press it in using a rubber spatula. Sprinkle the remaining crumble on top (it will be a little sticky). Serve with your choice of toppings if you like.

NOTE: You can toast your almonds if you like for extra flavor and crispness, though the recipe will no longer be raw. Either way is delicious.

SUPERCHARGE: Drink the fortified liquid from straining the applesauce for a live raw cider—dilute it with water or Water Kefir (page 42) if it's too sweet.

TART AND CRUNCHY APPLESAUCE

Makes 2 quarts (2 liters)

In addition to its featuring role in the Star Anise-Spiced Apple Crumble on page 181, this lively applesauce is perfect plain, straight from the fermenting jar. If you are serving it as a side to a meat entrée, adjust the seasonings to match the dish—for example, omitting the star anise to go with the pork chops on page 158.

2 lemons

4 pounds (1.75 kilograms; about 7) apples

1/4 cup (50 grams) packed unrefined dark brown sugar

1 teaspoon ground star anise

1/2 teaspoon ground cinnamon

1/4 teaspoon freshly grated nutmeg

1 teaspoon fine sea salt

Pinch of freshly ground black pepper

1/4 cup (60 milliliters) Water Kefir (page 42) or other starter culture (optional; page 20)

Fill a bowl with water and squeeze the juice from one of the lemons into the bowl. Add the squeezed lemon halves to the bowl too. Peel the apples if you like, core them, and coarsely chop, putting the pieces in the bowl of acidulated water as you go. Drain the apples, transfer them to a food processor, add the juice from the remaining lemon, and process to chunky applesauce texture. Return to the bowl and stir in the remaining ingredients. Pack into two 1-quart (1-liter) glass jars, leaving at least 1 inch (2.5 centimeters) of space remaining at the top. Cover tightly with a lid or airlock (page 19), place over a rimmed plate, and leave to ferment in a cool place away from sunlight for 1 to 3 days, until bubbly and tangy to your liking. Cover and refrigerate until ready to use.

HONEY-PICKLED FENNEL

Makes about 1/2 cup (120 grams)

I've chosen this recipe to close the book, first because it's a perfect sweet tidbit to serve at the end of any meal (both the fennel and honey are transformed as they ferment, resulting in a "pickled" fruit that works as a digestive aid), and second because it was shared with me by *Whole Foods Encyclopedia* author Rebecca Wood, a treasured friend and endless source of inspiration to me.

3/4 cup (60 grams) fennel bulb slices, including stalk and fronds

1/4 cup (60 milliliters) unpasteurized honey

Put the fennel in a medium glass jar and pour in the honey. Cover and set aside at room temperature for 12 to 18 hours, stirring after 1 hour or so when the honey has thinned.

To serve, lift fennel slices onto a small condiment plate, allowing several slices per person. Refrigerate the remainder and plan to use within the next 48 hours; though it will not spoil, the honey will continue to draw liquid from the fennel and after 4 days it will shrivel and toughen.

After you've finished the fennel pickles, you may use the now-thinned and lightly fennel-flavored honey for a second batch of pickles, to sweeten tea, or for another culinary purpose.

RESOURCES

PREPARED PICKLES, SAUERKRAUT, AND OTHER FERMENTS

Barry's Tempeh
www.growninbrooklyn.com
718-321-3211
Live and unpasteurized tempeh, sold in the freezer section in New York City area stores

Brassica and Brine
www.brassicaandbrine.com
Lactofermented foods sourced from local farms, based in Los Angeles

The Brinery
www.thebrinery.com
734-717-4469
Inventive lactofermented pickles available in the Michigan area

Cultured Pickle Shop
www.culturedpickleshop.com
510-540-5185
Berkeley, California–based specialty pickle shop

Fab Ferments
www.fabulousferments.com
513-562-7531
Krauts and such in the Ohio and Kentucky area

Farmer's Daughter
www.farmersdaughterbrand.com
919-259-3946
Collard kraut and other delights in the Piedmont area of North Carolina

Farmhouse Culture
www.farmhouseculture.com
831-466-0499
Sauerkraut in a variety of flavors from classic caraway to horseradish leek and kimchi; available nationally

Farmstead Ferments
www.farmsteadferments.com
540-718-3200
Krauts, kefir sodas, and chutney in the Virginia and D.C. area

Firefly Kitchens
www.fireflykitchens.com
206-436-8399
Kimchi, kraut, and other fermented items available in the Pacific Northwest

Fizzeology
www.fizzeology.com
608-638-FIZZ
Raw cultured foods in Wisconsin

The Gefilteria
www.gefilteria.com
347-688-8561
Beet kvass; available in New York City region, as well as Philadelphia, Columbus, Ohio, and Los Angeles

Gold Mine Natural Food Company
www.goldminenaturalfoods.com
800-475-3663
Sauerkraut, pickles, kimchi; Ohsawa products including pickled ginger, miso, umeboshi plums, paste, and vinegar, and sea vegetables

GT's Kombucha
www.synergydrinks.com
Kombucha in a variety of flavors; available nationally

Hawthorne Valley
www.hawthornevalleyfarm.org
518-672-7500
Biodynamic farm producing sauerkraut in a variety of flavors, fermented hot sauce, yogurt; available in the Northeast and at the Union Square Greenmarket in Manhattan

Hidden Pond Farm
www.hiddenpondllc.com
765-960-5092
Krauts, kvass, and tonics in Indiana and other parts of the Midwest

Katalyst Kombucha
www.katalystkombucha.com
413-773-9700
East Coast–based kombucha in a variety of flavors

Number 1 Sons
www.number1sons.com
202-570-4453
Kimchi, krauts, and pickles in the D.C. area

OlyKraut
www.olykraut.com
360-956-1048
Sauerkraut available in a variety of flavors including spicy garlic chi and sea vegetable; available in the Pacific Northwest

Organic Valley
www.organicvalley.coop
888-444-6455
Cultured butter and sour cream; available nationally

Pickled Planet
www.pickledplanet.com
541-201-2689
Sauerkraut, cucumber pickles, dilly beans, kimchi; available in Oregon, Washington, and California

Picklopolis
www.picklopolis.com
503-753-3477
Lactofermented pickles and hot sauces from Portland, Oregon

Real Pickles
www.realpickles.com
413-774-2600
Pickles and sauerkraut in a variety
of flavors, kimchi, ginger carrots,
beets, tomatillo hot sauce, beet kvass;
available in the Northeast

South River Miso Company
www.southrivermiso.com
413-369-4057
Hand-crafted artisan organic miso in
the Japanese farmhouse tradition

Spirit Creek Farm
www.spiritcreekfarm.com
715-742-3551
Sauerkraut, kimchi, and other
vegetable ferments based in
Wisconsin and serving the Midwest

Thirty Acre Farm
www.thirtyacrefarm.com
207-549-5384
A small farm making its own krauts in
Maine

Vermont Creamery
www.vermontcreamery.com
800-884-6287
Cultured butter and crème fraîche

Wake Robin Fermented Foods
www.wakerobinfoods.com
Lactofermented foods in the
Cleveland area

Zukay Live Foods
www.zukay.com
Kvass in a variety of flavors from the
standard beet to kvass flavored with
berries, turmeric, and melon; available
nationally

SPICES, FLAVORINGS, SEA VEGETABLES, AND OTHER PANTRY INGREDIENTS

Bob's Red Mill
www.bobsredmill.com
503-654-3215
Teff grain and flour and other quality
grains

Celtic Sea Salt
www.celticseasalt.com
800-867-7258
Mineral-rich unprocessed sea salt

Eden Foods
www.edenfoods.com
888-424-3336
Trusted source of organic products
including sea vegetables, umeboshi
plums and paste, spices, herbs, and
grains

Kalustyan's
www.kalustyans.com
800-352-3451
Specialty food shop offering a wide
variety of seasonings including
berbere, preserved lemon, and many
hard-to-find ingredients

Maine Coast Sea Vegetables
www.seaveg.com
207-565-2907
Sustainably harvested sea vegetables

Maine Sea Salt Company
www.maineseasalt.com
207-255-3310
Unprocessed, solar-evaporated sea
salt

Maskal Teff
www.teffco.com
888-822-2221
Teff grain and flour

**Medicine Flower Aromatic
Apothecary**
www.medicineflower.com
800-787-3645
Organic, cold-pressed extracts in
unique flavors such as white cherry
and guava

Mendocino Sea Vegetable Company
www.seaweed.net
707-895-2996
The first cottage craft seaweed
company

Mountain Rose Herbs
www.mountainroseherbs.com
800-879-3337
Good selection of organic spices

Penzeys Spices
www.penzeys.com
800-741-7787
Wide variety of spices including
berbere seasoning

COCONUT PRODUCTS

Edward & Sons
www.edwardandsons.com
Native Forest brand organic canned
coconut milk and coconut cream

Exotic Superfoods
www.exoticsuperfoods.com
917-685-2586 or 347-804-3961
Frozen organic young Thai coconut
meat and coconut water

FERMENTATION STARTERS AND EQUIPMENT

Counter Culture Pottery
www.counterculturepottery.com
Handcrafted fermentation crocks

Cultures for Health
www.culturesforhealth.com
800-962-1959
Buttermilk, kefir, kombucha, Water
Kefir, and yogurt starters; airlocks;
fermentation kits; kraut pounders;
yogurt makers and food dehydrators;
fermentation crocks and fermentation
tools

Excalibur
www.excaliburdehydrator.com
800-875-4254
Food dehydrators with removable
shelves and thermostat

Farm Curious
www.farmcurious.com
510-410-3761
Fermentation crocks, fermentation
sets with airlocks

GEM Cultures
www.gemcultures.com
253-588-2922
Kefir, kombucha, and water kefir
starters

GI ProHealth
www.giprohealth.com
774-328-2472
Dairy and nondairy yogurt starters

Kombucha Brooklyn
www.kombuchabrooklyn.com
917-261-3010
Kombucha-making supplies and kits

Ogusky Ceramics
www.clayrocks.com
Handcrafted fermentation crocks

Ohio Stoneware
www.ohiostoneware.com
740-450-4415
Pickling crocks

Pickl-It
www.pickl-it.com
603-722-0189
Airlock system for fermentation

Williams-Sonoma
www.williams-sonoma.com
877-812-6235
Pickling crocks and kits, yogurt makers

Yolife
www.yolifeyogurt.com
888-254-7336
Yogurt makers

FURTHER READING

The Art of Fermentation: An In-Depth Exploration of Essential Concepts and Processes from Around the World, by Sandor Ellix Katz

The Essential Book of Fermentation: Great Taste and Good Health with Probiotic Foods, by Jeff Cox

The Kimchi Cookbook: 60 Traditional and Modern Ways to Make and Eat Kimchi, by Lauryn Chun

Kombucha! The Amazing Probiotic Tea That Cleanses, Heals, Energizes, and Detoxifies, by Eric and Jessica Childs

Mastering Fermentation: Recipes for Making and Cooking with Fermented Foods, by Mary Karlin

The New Whole Foods Encyclopedia: An A to Z of Selection, Preparation, and Storage for More Than 1,000 Common and Uncommon Fruits, Vegetables, Grains, and Herbs, by Rebecca Wood

The Nourished Kitchen: Farm-to-Table Recipes for the Traditional Foods Lifestyle, by Jennifer McGruther

Nourishing Traditions: The Cookbook That Challenges Politically Correct Nutrition and the Diet Dictocrats, by Sally Fallon

Wild Fermentation: The Flavor, Nutrition, and Craft of Live-Culture Foods, by Sandor Ellix Katz

WEBSITES AND BLOGS

Cultures for Health
www.culturesforhealth.com
Comprehensive database of
fermentation instructions and recipes

Fermenters Club
www.fermentersclub.com
Fermentation community with
newsletter and recipes

Leda's Kitchen
www.ledaskitchen.com
Creative recipes with a focus on
fermented foods

Nourished Kitchen
www.nourishedkitchen.com
Traditional foods site with many
fermentation recipes

Rebecca Wood
www.rebeccawood.com
Whole foods pioneer's site including
a variety of health topics and
fermentation recipes

Weston A. Price Foundation
www.westonaprice.org
Traditional foods site with information
on nutrient-dense foods including
fermented foods, traditional broth,
and raw milk

Wild Fermentation
www.wildfermentation.com
Fermentation revivalist Sandor Katz's
site, with innovative recipes and links
for further research

ACKNOWLEDGMENTS

I was gifted with not one but two wonderful editors at Rizzoli. The vision for this book was born out of a lunch with Christopher Steighner, senior editor and head of the cookbook division, and Martynka Wawrzyniak joined Chris in spearheading the project. The two were involved both professionally and personally to a degree I never could imagined. Chris's vision and refined editorial skills and Martynka's engagement and passion for fermentation have made this book what it is.

Also at Rizzoli, thank you to production manager Colin Hough-Trapp for guiding the book through its many stages, publicist Nicki Clendening for promoting the book, and publisher Charles Miers for giving me the opportunity to join the distinguished Rizzoli roster.

To the team who put the subject of fermentation into a gorgeous coffee table book: William Brinson is the best photographer I could have hoped for to work on this project. Food stylist Suzanne Lenzer put together the plates in a sophisticated and most impressive way. Stephanie Hanes, prop stylist, was integral in setting the stage for the shots. Many thanks to Jan Derevjanik for the elegant book design. And to Elizabeth Ungerleider for shooting my author photo.

To Sandor Katz for writing the foreword to this book, giving the manuscript a close read, and, most of all, bringing fermentation back to its important place in our culture with *Wild Fermentation* and *The Art of Fermentation*.

To Sally Fallon Morell for leading the traditional foods revival with her seminal *Nourishing Traditions*.

To cookbook author, food justice activist, and cooking school friend Bryant Terry for his kind words.

To Rebecca Wood, mentor, friend, and inspiration for pursuing a career in food. Our friendship was sealed over an edition of *The New Whole Foods Encyclopedia* when I was a managing editor at Penguin Books, and we have been collaborators ever since. I couldn't have written this book without her.

For recipes: Thank you to Rebecca Wood for the Cherry Bounce and Honey-Pickled Fennel recipes and Patricia Austin for her Devilish Cupcakes. To Julia Wawrzyniak for the idea for the Misomite recipe and Natalia Potocka for the pickle salad suggestion. To Nash Patel for the Indian recipes. To Martynka Wawrzyniak for testing many recipes and generously sharing from her own repertoire, in particular her almond yogurt and coconut yogurt recipes, and Chris Steighner for his multiple recipe suggestions, in particular the pork chops.

In the kitchen: Thank you to Cindy Hebbard, who shared freely of her knowledge of fermentation. And to Ariel Scheintaub, Meryl Mastrocinque, Gabriel Weiss, and Coridon Bratton for their help prepping, and trying out recipes.

Thank you to old friends who are always enthusiastic about my books and game for taste testing: Cindy Achar, Janice Baldwin, Jerry Ann and Patti Jacobs, Sharon Katzmann, Suzy LeFevre, Denise McDermott, Mary Thill, Susan VanOmmeren, and Pamela Vittorio. Having good friends makes for an inspired life.

Thank you to my brother, Ross Scheintaub, and his family for their encouragement.

Special acknowledgment goes to three food friends, my go-to people for all things recipes and publishing. To Liana Krissoff, a cookbook author with whom I've collaborated on many projects and the first person I go to when I've got culinary news to share; she also copyedited the manuscript for this book and gave indispensible advice along the way. To Marisa Bulzone, a wealth of knowledge on the ins and outs of the publishing business, who has generously shared advice with me whenever a new project arises. And to Patricia Austin, whose impeccable taste, discernment, and shared values have enriched my life both in and out of the kitchen since moving from New York to Vermont.

To my mother and father, who have given me the love and confidence to pursue my varied and changing dreams.

And to my husband and dining partner, Nash Patel, who brings sweetness into my life.

INDEX